YANKEE

YANKEE

The Inside Story of
a Champion Bloodhound

ROGER A. CARAS

G.P. Putnam's Sons
New York

Copyright © 1979 by Roger A. Caras
All rights reserved. Published
simultaneously in Canada by
Longman Canada Limited, Toronto.
Printed in the United States of America

Library of Congress Cataloging in Publication Data

Caras, Roger A
Yankee.
SUMMARY: An animal lover and professional natural-
ist describes his family's adventures in raising
a personable bloodhound into a champion show dog.
1. Bloodhounds—Legends and stories. 2. Bloodhounds—Juvenile literature. 3. Caras, Roger A.—
Juvenile literature. [1. Bloodhounds. 2. Caras,
Roger A] I. Title.

SF429.B6C37   1979   636.7'53   79-12133
ISBN 0-399-20688-4

For Jill—who agrees that woman came
from the rib of a man, but who insists that
man came from the rib of a bloodhound. . .
and for Jackie and Sink,
where it all started.

One

It was an unseasonably hot Sunday in October. That was back in 1974. Earlier that morning Rebby had seemed nervous. (Her real name was Champion The Rectory's Rebel Yell.) It had been sixty-three days since Rebby had been mated to another great Rectory dog, Champion The Rectory's Wisdom, whose *call name* was R. J. Most show dogs do have two names: the long one appears in show programs and the other is the familiar name used around their homes. Very few dogs know to answer to their fancy show names. If anyone had called out, "Here, Champion The Rectory's Rebel Yell, here," she would have looked at them in amazement. "Here, Rebby," on the other hand, was guaranteed to bring a lot of tail thumping and a big jowly smile.

The Rectory dogs are bloodhounds, large animals that can weigh as much as 150 pounds. Most are reddish brown with a black saddle mark on their backs, a few are liver-colored or fawn, and fewer yet are all glossy black with tan face markings like R. J.

The kennel known as The Rectory got its name in a very logical way. Although it is now located in a wilderness area outside Farmington, Maine, it originally grew up in the backyard of St. Thomas's Rectory in Owings Mills, Maryland, right on church grounds. The people who started it all were the Reverend and Mrs. George Sinkinson—Jackie and Sink to their friends.

On that October morning Jackie was in London and Sink was alone with the dogs at the rectory. When he saw Rebby moving from one side of the room to the other after being still for less than a minute each time, he could only groan, "Oh, no! Not now!" He had to get to the church and conduct morning services, and Rebby looked as if she would start to give birth at any moment. Frantically, Sink dialed Dr. Bob Patterson's phone number. He was The Rectory's veterinarian, but he was already out on an emergency call. A cow was giving birth that morning too. It seemed to Sink as if the whole world were having babies as he rushed into his vestments and hurried across the parking lot to greet the early-arriving churchgoers. He was sure he looked very undignified and couldn't remember whether or not he had brushed his hair. When he looked down he was relieved to see the tips of his black shoes showing, for he wasn't sure he had changed out of his bedroom slippers.

Sink shook hands, smiled, shook some more hands, and then dashed off. With his startled parishioners staring after him, he ran back to the rectory. Rebby was already seeing to her first puppy. Sink checked to be sure it was alive, and then tried Bob Patterson's phone again. This time it was busy. He rolled his eyes heavenward and thought for a moment how lucky people are who can swear at times like this. Of course, one never knows exactly what a minister is saying when he mumbles to himself.

Back at the church, Father Sinkinson launched into the service with what appeared to be remarkable nervous energy. During a hymn—he chose a nice long one and hissed instructions for the organist to keep it going as long as possible—he ran back to the house and found Rebby with her second puppy. Both were black, since all bloodhounds are born dark, and those that are destined to be light in color change during their first three to six months. This time Bob Patterson's phone rang—and rang—and rang. Back in the church the congregation began whispering and looking around nervously as the organist launched into the same hymn for a third round. Finally a disheveled Father George Sinkinson strode down the aisle wearing a sheepish grin. Dr. Patterson was on his way, and the first two puppies were doing fine. That morning the Reverend Mr. Sinkinson delivered a stirring sermon on the miracle of life and why we never should take it for granted.

After church services, Sink and Dr. Patterson hovered over Rebby as she struggled to deliver her third puppy. Something was wrong, and they decided to get her to the animal hospital as quickly as possible. The puppies were bundled in towels and put on the back seat of Dr. Patterson's car next to their mother. Rebby simply would not tolerate their being left behind; so, rather than make her more nervous than she already was, they kept her babies with her. She kept sniffing the towels, uncovering the puppies, and bathing them with her tongue while Dr. Patterson worked his way through Sunday traffic and Sink nervously watched mother and babies.

In the hospital, Rebby was placed under anesthesia and a Caesarean section performed. That is, instead of her puppies being born in the usual way, they were removed through an incision in her abdomen. Eight more bloodhound puppies were born to The Rectory Kennels that Sunday before the last churchgoer sat down to Sunday lunch.

The fifth puppy born that morning, the third to be removed during the Caesarean operation, was a strong little male with enough skin to hold two puppies. He would one day earn the name Champion The Rectory's Yankee Patriot. The world would know him as Yankee, and he would be seen by millions of television viewers and dog show spectators. That morning, though, there was just a lot of squirming, kicking, and pushing as he fought his litter mates to find a food supply. There were very few signs of a great champion in those first hours.

Because Rebby had had surgery, she was not given her puppies to nurse that first night. Dr. Patterson and Father Sinkinson slipped tubes down the puppies' throats and fed them the formula that would keep them alive until Rebby could handle the task of feeding the ten pushy babies herself. By the time the puppies had been given their first meal and moved back to the rectory, Sink was upset, nervous, and tired. His stomach was bothering him, too, for he had not eaten all day. Throughout the evening friends and members of his congregation called and dropped by to see how he and his dogs were doing.

Late that night, after the puppies had been fed and bedded down in the large warm container known as a whelping box, Sink collapsed in a chair. He decided to have a drink since he was too excited to sleep. Then the phone rang, and he learned that the kennel had taken new honors that day. R. J.'s mother, Champion The Rectory's Reward, and also Rebby's half-sister, had won two important ribbons on the day her ten grandchildren—they were also her half-nieces and half-nephews—were born. Although it had been strenuous on humans, Yankee's birthday had been a happy one for bloodhounds. As for Yankee himself, he slept 22½ out of his first 24 hours on earth as an independent, free-breathing companion of man.

Not all breeds of dog produce puppies that look like miniature adults, but bloodhounds do. There is no way that you can mistake a bloodhound, no matter how small it is. Since the breed has looked much as it does now for almost 2,500 years, the design is well established. It is a cross between a noble bronze statue and a cartoon character. What is a bloodhound really like? What would Yankee have to grow up to be if he was to become a credit to his breed and his kennel?

First, bloodhounds—and this includes the puppies—seem to have too much skin. They can almost turn around inside their own outer covering. There is a reason for that. When a bloodhound is on the trail—and that is where bloodhounds belong—they will stop at nothing. Wherever the trail leads they will go. (Some people describe this trait as tenacity, others as stupidity.) Very often, trails lead through brambles, thickets, and, in modern times, barbed wire fences. A tight-skinned dog can get hung up on obstacles like that while a loose-skinned dog such as a bloodhound can twist out of anything. They are, in fact, almost impossible to hold when they want to wriggle free. A bloodhound with business to attend to is like a sack of snakes. You just can't get a grip, except on the tail.

In the show ring that loose skin is called a *cape.* It is expected to be free and full of wrinkles. (The newborn puppies don't actually have their wrinkles, but they are born with lines where the wrinkles will eventually go. The wrinkles, then, are preordained.) When a bloodhound drops his nose to the ground to follow a trail, the cape slips forward and makes it difficult for him to see where he is going. That usually isn't too much of a hardship, since as scent hounds they follow their noses anyway. The problem is that bloodhounds are always bumping into things. The first time someone walks a bloodhound on a city street it can be quite surprising. *Bong! Bonk! Thud!* It is the canine version of the Anvil Chorus. The great hounds walk into fender after fender as they move along enjoying the symphony of smells that is to them a city street. After a while bloodhound owners get to know the different makes of cars by the sounds the fenders make. Some American cars are really tinny sounding. Peugeots and Rolls-Royces sound like tanks. Bloodhounds would make terrible seeing-eye dogs.

A second characteristic of the true bloodhound is what the people in the dog show world call *leather*. That doesn't mean feet or leashes, but those great, long ears. All true bloodhounds are supposed to have leather (ears) that hang well below their noses. There is a reason for that, too. The trail a bloodhound follows is made up of billions of tiny particles that break free from the skin of people as they move. The faster a person walks or runs the more the tiny scent particles are likely to break free and fall to the ground. It is like invisible dandruff. People don't like to think of themselves as shedding, but they do.

On a cold, damp day those scent particles settle to the ground. On a warm, dry day they rise up and float above the ground. If the day is damp and cold and a bloodhound is on the trail he brings his ears into play. Instinctively he knows to swirl his ears around by moving his head back and forth. The ear tips, hanging below the nose, move the particles up into the great bloodhound nose chamber. It is a very old system, and it works.

Also, bloodhound disposition is terribly important. Old movies often show bloodhounds thundering through the forest in great, free-running, madly bellowing packs trying to find someone to tear apart. That is all nonsense. Bloodhounds are used alone, not in packs, and they are never used off lead. Since a bloodhound will not look up when he is on a hot trail (remember the fender chorus in the city!), he has no road sense at all. A bloodhound, once on a good stinky trail, will walk across the busiest turnpike in the world and never look to left or right. That is one reason why the great hounds are kept on long leads. The other is that the handler could never keep up with his dog. Of course, bloodhounds trail silently. When the handler is after a criminal, the last thing he wants to do when moving through the woods at night is to announce where he is. The other fellow might have a gun!

The silliest fiction about bloodhounds, though, concerns their hunting down and tearing their human victims apart. Bloodhounds are never trained to attack. They are much too gentle for that. They hunt human beings, to be sure, but to them it is a game. They are hunting down a human being not to attack him but to drool on him. Since bloodhounds are used to trail lost children and strayed campers far more often than to hunt escaped criminals, it would make no sense to have a dog that promptly ate the trailee. Bloodhounds have always been bred for a calm and gentle nature. They love people, cats, other dogs, usually, and their comfort. They are very fond of human beds and prefer down to foam rubber pillows. They have style.

Where did such gentle dogs get such an awful name, then? Why *blood*hounds? In the Middle Ages, in England, there were two classes of hounds. One was meant to be owned by the common people, but one great hound could be owned only by people related to the royal family: it was the hound of the blood (meaning blueblood) or the blooded hound. It is not difficult to see how the breed's name evolved. We don't have many *bluebloods* today, but I think bloodhound owners still tend to regard themselves as being elevated by their hounds.

All of this tradition and advanced trailing design had been born in Yankee. It was nothing that interested him very much at the beginning. His eyes were sealed, his nose hadn't really begun to work very well, and, though loud noises could startle him, he was nearly deaf. All the sounds around him blended into a kind of hum. At the beginning there was the feeling of warmth from his littermates and his mother, Rebby, and the need to feed. When not sleepy, he seemed to be hungry all the time—and hunger to a new puppy is like pain. It is a problem that has to be solved immediately. It doesn't take a bloodhound puppy long to learn he can grunt. Then he learns to squeal. And that is what a bloodhound's first few days consist of: sleep, squeal, grunt, suck, sleep, squeal, grunt, suck.

Two

Yankee had a big job to do in those first days. He had to start the process of building bone and muscle. Like all large breeds, bloodhounds mature slowly. A male bloodhound isn't fully matured, doesn't have all of his great sturdy substance, until he is almost three years old. A much smaller dog, like a toy poodle or a papillon, will mature in fourteen months. If you think about it, that means a bloodhound has to do in three years what a human being will do in twenty or perhaps twenty-one years. It takes more than good intentions to do that.

It takes a lot of sucking and shoving to get enough food to keep on schedule, and Yankee set about his task with enormous enthusiasm. On the day he was born he could be cupped into two hands, easily. At twelve weeks he would weigh thirty pounds and be very difficult to pick up. Bloodhound puppies don't really have a center of gravity. There is simply no middle to them. They flow like cold prune juice. No matter where you grab them, they seem to be slipping and squishing the other way. You always end up with a lot of loose skin and a puppy that is yelping as if you were killing him. They are like pillowcases half filled with lead jellybeans. But Yankee had a way to go before he lost his center. It would be some time before he was anything but a digestive system with legs.

All puppies are attracted to heat. That is how they find their mother. Once they are there they know exactly what to do. They grab onto a nipple and try to bulldoze their way right through her abdomen while, at the same time, they push their littermates away with their feet. The combination of sucking, bulldozing, shoving, and humming is what life is all about—and it is exhausting. What level of patience it takes to be a bloodhound mother in the middle of that milk-soaked Roman arena cannot be imagined. There must be a special category of sainthood for bloodhound bitches.

Some scientists say newborn puppies (they are sometimes called *neonates* for the first thirty-six to forty-eight hours) are a little like reptiles and amphibians. They can't control their own body temperature as well as older puppies and dogs can, and so they have to be near their mothers in order to stay warm. It is perhaps one reason why puppies very often sleep in heaps. They like the security of other puppies against them, and it also helps them to keep their body temperature up to about 101 degrees Fahrenheit. That is the normal temperature for a healthy dog.

The whelping box into which Sink placed the puppies and into which Rebby was introduced a couple of days later was designed to keep mothers from rolling over on a sleeping puppy and suffocating it. Even the best of mothers can do that when there is nothing but wall-to-wall puppies in sight. The box is simple. It is high enough to keep the puppies in once they find their legs and decide the world is for exploring and chewing on, and it has a rail around the inside that keeps the mother toward the center. She can't roll against the walls, which is where a puppy could most readily be pinned and killed. There is often a heat lamp overhead.

Until Rebby was reintroduced to her puppies, Sink and Jackie fed each puppy every four hours around the clock. Jackie returned from London about twelve hours after the last puppy was born. She breezed through the door with a jolly, "Hi, Honey, what's new?" While the cab driver stared in amazement, the Reverend George Sinkinson, barefoot, white Episcopalian priest's collar half on and half off, formula dripping down his black pants, with a squirming, grunting bloodhound puppy under one arm while he tried to feed it with the other hand, told her. Then they both began to laugh and went off to see the rest of the puppies. Several minutes later they remembered the cab driver. He was still in the kitchen. He accepted his tip, nodded, and moved out the back door mumbling something about how nice it was to be a Methodist.

To understand Yankee's first days and weeks you have to understand the Sinkinsons. Sink is very tall and powerful. He has a minister's voice and a lumberjack's build. He looks as if sinning around him could be dangerous. But he is soft and gentle most of the time. Jackie is quite short, but makes up for it in other ways. Since both Jackie and Sink have been handling bloodhounds for years, their arms are extremely strong. Bloodhounds, it seems, have been leading people to where they want to go (even when they haven't known where it was they wanted to go) for over two thousand years. Bloodhounds have never been able to figure out why people would want them if they already knew where they should be headed. So bloodhounds pull and pull and pull. It is very hard to teach one of these great beasts that they should go where the human at the other end of the lead is going at about the same pace the human wants to move. Tug-of-war doesn't really describe the action since the dogs are so peaceful; perhaps tug-of-peace is better.

Jackie is not a terribly quiet person. As a matter of fact, some of her friends have wondered if she was a marine drill sergeant in a former life. Actually she is as gentle as Sink, but a little noisier. She loves her dogs, she loves Sink, and she loves their children. She also loves to roar at all of them. Sometimes they all roar back at the same time. Jackie is an ongoing thunderstorm, all heart, very generous, very loyal, but a thunderstorm just the same. She would have been an incredible evangelist, or hog-caller.

Yankee's nose was the first of his senses to start coming into focus. By the third day the humming sound around him had begun to take on distinctive features. Jackie's voice, as she leaned over the whelping box (which was almost all the time), was different to him from the squealing of one of the other puppies. But even before that much sound came into focus there were the sounds his mother made, the purring sound when the puppies nursed, and then there were the sweet, rolling, baying sounds the other hounds made in the kennels and runs nearby.

Yankee's mother had a distinctive smell. The area around her nipples was a mixture of sweet and sour from slurped milk and puppy spit. Jackie and Sink had their own smells and the clean air outside the whelping box was very different from the deep, earthy dog-smell inside the six-by-eight-foot enclosure. Yankee quickly registered those smells. Inside his head he had a kind of computer that would always enable him to record a smell and keep it separate from all other smells in the world. A bloodhound can pick one person out of tens of thousands and almost never become confused. They say a bloodhound's nose is at least two million times as sensitive as a person's. That is probably a good thing because the bloodhound muzzle, with its great chambers where smells are sorted out, would not go well on the front of a human head.

Once Yankee's nose and ears were in focus, the world expanded. From the beginning, of course, there had been the sense of touch and heat that had helped him feed. Then, after a week, small, pale slivers of light began penetrating under his lids. It was then that Yankee's world really began to take form.

Small puppies are rather like wrinkled sausages. They are all stomach and, in the case of bloodhounds, ears. They have legs, of course, but they are not strong enough to push the pup up in the air where it belongs. Very little sunlight passes beneath a bloodhound puppy in that first week. When they want to travel (and four or five feet is virtually a trip abroad) they use their legs to push. They have sharp little needle nails and they dig into whatever they touch. They push, squirm, and wriggle like seals out on the ice. Sometimes the nails dig into the soft padding on the floor of the whelping box, sometimes into the stomach of the poor, patient bitch, but usually they dig into another puppy's ear, nose, or eyes. That is why there is so much squealing in the whelping box. At age one week, a puppy doesn't know how to bark, snarl, or bite, but it knows how to squeal in pain and anger. No grudges are held. A puppy has an attention span of about one-tenth of a second.

As Yankee's eyes began to let the light in, he became more and more aware of his surroundings. Each hour the world seemed to roll back. It was like peeling a piece of delicious fruit. It was all there, all born fresh and new just for him. There were his littermates. He had been crawling over, under, and around them for days and nights, but they never really began to take on personalities of their own until touch, smell, taste, sound, and sight all began working together in harmony to create a complete impression. One thing he found: when his mother was out of the whelping box and he felt like a little snack, his littermates had delicious ears. They weren't very nourishing, but with his teeth coming in and his stomach always grumbling, even puppy ears were better than nothing. Soon all were doing it and there wasn't a dry ear in the house. As their teeth erupted through their gums (they were as sharp as common pins) there was yet another excuse for squealing. Bloodhounds hate having their ears bitten almost as much as they like biting other hounds' ears.

Although Jackie had not been present at the birth of this Yankee litter (all the puppies were given Yankee as a first name, and our Yankee, hero of this book, was Yankee Patriot), she was quickly in charge of puppy care at The Rectory. It did not bother Sink at all to let control slip from his hands. It meant he could start seeing to the needs of his human flock again. There were weddings, funerals, christenings, and all the other things that normally go on in and around churches. Sink listened to his human charges as they fussed and fumed over the vicissitudes of life while Jackie listened to the bloodhound equivalent in the whelping box. It is not easy, she observed late one night, to be a puppy. There is so much to do in such a short time. And so much is expected of you when you are from ancient, honorable, championship stock. Often, in the evenings, when all the chores of church and kennel were done, Jackie and Sink would stand beside the whelping box and just look. You don't have to be religious, they observed, to know a miracle when you see one. And if a bloodhound puppy isn't a miracle, what on earth is?

Three

When Yankee was four weeks old, he and his littermates began their first short excursions away from the whelping box room. They were toddlers by then, able to walk, however unsteadily, from one side of a room to the other. The first time Yankee was put down in the large living room of the rectory, he showed his appreciation by spreading his back knees slightly, lowering his backside just a little, and piddling. He was rushed out the door still dripping and put onto the grass. The grass smelled so very different from anything he had ever smelled before he forgot all about his immediate business and began sniffing.

It isn't really possible for a human being to understand what a bloodhound experiences when he is introduced to a new smell. I suppose we could draw a rough analogy. When a bloodhound lowers his nose to smell grass where people and other dogs have been it is like you and me, with cotton in our ears, walking up to someone who is whistling. If we removed the cotton and heard the sound of a full symphony orchestra coming from the whistler's lips, we would have some idea of what it must be like to smell things two million times as acutely as we now do. That is what Yankee experienced out there on the soft grass. Every human being and dog that had come that way since the last rain was still there in scent-memory. Yankee was far too young to find any meaning in the signals he was snuffling in, but it certainly was interesting. He found out what all bloodhounds must come to know. Smelling new smells is a great way to pass time and a lot better than coming when you are called or doing anything else you are told to do by a mere person.

Yankee had no sense of time, nor does any other dog. Days and nights come and go, and they mean nothing. It is just as nice to sleep all·day and be a pest all night as the other way around. The only markers in time are meals; that is especially so when you are still a very young dog. As Yankee grew, though, there was another marker—the time outside. After a few experimental, well-supervised trips the puppies began spending the warm hours of the day out on a fenced grassy plot. The big Rectory dogs were up a slope, away from the house. Although the puppies could hear their magnificent voices, they were still apart, things yet to be discovered and chewed.

The original supervision of the puppies on the grass was to determine if there were any pebble hounds in the litter. It is not possible to remove every pebble, twig, and blowing leaf from a large enclosure, and some puppies do make themselves sick by swallowing all kinds of weird things. Years later, in fact, one of Yankee's cousins would die because, even as an adult dog, he could not be discouraged from gulping down every stone and piece of rubbish he came upon. The puppies, though, were watched carefully and their outside play area kept as clean as possible. When they couldn't find anything else worth chewing on, they always had each others' tails and ears. At times they formed an undulating chain, with each clamped onto the tail or ear of another. There was a lot of squealing and early-stage growling when these chewy chains took form. They usually collapsed into a large harmless brawl and no one really was hurt.

By the time they were four weeks old, Rebby decided it had all been a dreadful mistake. Puppies, she seemed to be thinking, were a terrible idea. She had been bitten, scratched, pushed, and mauled to the very end of her endurance. She began warning the puppies away when they got too rough or too competitive. The puppies learned an important new fact about life. There were rules. Someone or something could and would tell them what to do, and they would have to do it. It didn't take long for Yankee to learn that when Rebby growled, "Enough of that!" it was safer to listen than to ignore her. Rebby would never bite her own puppies, but she was capable of knocking them over and making perfectly terrible sounds.

The first time Rebby charged into Yankee with a great warning roar, Yankee discovered something new within himself. It was the instinctive knowledge of how to be submissive. This is a pattern of behavior that all dogs must understand if they are to get along with one another. There can be only one top dog. When two dogs think they are on the top, a serious fight can ensue. Rebby was dominant, she *was* top dog (technically, of couse, top bitch) in the puppy enclosure. She was the pack leader, and her growl was law. When she singled out one puppy and butted it while making the warning sounds, the puppy was expected to roll over and stick its chin out while whining in a special way. That whine and that pose, with the neck stretched out for the dominant dog to bite, means "I surrender to you." Rebby, of course, would never accept the offer and bite the exposed throat. No dominant dog ever does as long as the submission ritual is played out. That is why few dog fights end in death unless one of the dogs is crazy or they are very unevenly matched in size. All a dog has to do to end a fight is enact the submission ritual. All of Rebby's puppies learned how to do that. The day would come when Yankee would expect submission from other dogs. That day, though, was still a long way off.

The days and weeks passed easily in the Maryland countryside. After the puppies were weaned, there was never the feeling of real hunger again. They were fed on the ad-lib schedule many scientifically run kennels use today. A bowl of specially balanced puppy ration is always available. Later in life hounds eat according to a strict regimen, but as puppies they always have food and water on hand. The schedule is usually to play a few minutes, munch a little food, play a little, munch a little more food, and then plop into the water dish and spill it. Keeping a bowl full of water in an enclosure full of bloodhound puppies is an endless task. Of course, you can always use heavy, weighted dishes that are much wider at the bottom than at the top. Puppies can't tip them over as easily, but they can lie in them.

A word on puppy food: apparently it tastes awful and the owner must be very careful not to let the puppy taste other food. As long as the recently weaned pup thinks all solid food tastes terrible, it will eat because it must. Once it discovers that other foods taste swell, forget about scientifically balanced puppy food. The trick is to live the lie as long as you can.

Since bloodhounds are expected to be pleasant, gentle dogs, a very important process begins the day they are born and continues until they leave the kennel, if the kennel is a good one. The process is known as socialization. The puppies are picked up, held, cuddled, played with, and taken away from the company of other dogs at least once a day and often many more times than that. They quickly become accustomed to the idea that human contact means pleasure, that human beings are friends. In time they come to crave human companionship more than any other kind.

Yankee wasn't at all hard to convince. There were Jackie and Sink, whose hands were strong and seemed to control the world. There were guests, who weren't as reliably strong as Jackie and Sink, but they all smelled different and that was interesting. The other familiar hands belonged to Dr. Patterson. He was often there, and his hands were very positive in their approach. Mouths got pried open; tonsils and ear canals got looked at; bellies got squished and prodded; there were small indignities back aft, under the tail; toes got spread; and every now and then a whole big bunch of skin got pulled up on the back of the neck and there was a quick pricking sensation. Bloodhounds have so much skin they usually don't mind needles after the first time or two. Yankee didn't seem to pay any attention to them at all. He couldn't understand what was happening, of course, but he was being protected against a whole range of diseases that could strike him down as a puppy, or even as an adult dog, and leave him a physical wreck if he survived at all. Every night Jackie and Sink pried his mouth open and pushed a pill far down into his throat. With his muzzle held upright, his throat was stroked until he swallowed. He soon learned that the quicker he swallowed his heart worm pill, the sooner he could go back and bite someone's tail. Physical examinations, shots, pills, they all became part of the ritual of life. Bloodhounds are usually very good about such matters. As adults they stand as still as mountains. It is doubtful that any dog can understand a concept as difficult as "this is for your own good," but bloodhounds seem to.

Four

Although Yankee and his littermates never understood what was happening, their group began to shrink. One by one puppies were taken out of the play area and did not come back. Something besides socialization was going on. Reluctantly the Sinkinsons were selling their bloodhound babies of the Yankee litter to very select homes.

One puppy was what is known as "pet-quality." That meant that, although it might be the nicest hound in the whole world, its ears were a little short or its legs a little long; or for some other reason it would not do well in the show ring and would not make the kind of breeding stock that bloodhounds need. This puppy, at less than half the cost of the show-quality dogs, went to a good home that had been checked out and approved. The people did not want a show dog, but they did want a bloodhound. They admired the breed very much. It was agreed they could have the pup but would never breed it. It was to be spayed. They could use it for trailing, though. A bloodhound does not have to be beautiful on the outside to have a talented nose. The scent-sorting genius that makes bloodhounds superior to all other trailing breeds is tucked away inside.

Jackie and Sink held back a few special puppies, but the others went, each a potential champion. One at a time, homes of applicants were checked out; usually the people themselves came to visit the Maryland kennel, and the puppies' ownership changed. At birth the puppies had been registered with the American Kennel Club in New York City. The facts of their birth and parentage were stored in the computers along with information on millions of other dogs. As each puppy left the Sinkinson kennel a new form was submitted to the AKC and the computer on Madison Avenue kicked out a new slip with a name that was approved. It had to be a name that no other living dog bore. Only with signed permission from the Sinkinsons could the words *The Rectory's* appear in the pup's name. A kennel lets its name be registered only when the owners feel the dog is truly representative of their standards, their efforts to achieve perfection.

Many people don't seem to understand what pure-bred dogs are all about. A dog like a bloodhound carries with it a lot of human history. For almost twenty-five centuries people have been trying to build and protect an ideal hound through selective breeding. A fine, pure-bred dog that lives up to the expectations of its breeders is much more than a pet; it is an accomplishment. When a kennel allows its name to be used it means that that particular dog comes as close as can reasonably be expected to being what the kennel set out to do.

Yankee and two of his littermates were held back by Jackie and Sink for some months after the others had gone. They weren't sure they wanted to sell them at all, for they appeared to be extra special. But, in East Hampton, New York, another force in the life of Yankee was taking shape.

The Caras household is animal-oriented. My wife and I collect animal art, paintings and sculpture. We have, on the average, nine or ten dogs, five to ten cats, a horse or two, and snakes, tarantulas, and other animal guests. (I used to have two millipedes, but one got cut in half by a sliding terrarium top. The front half lived and I ended up with a millipede and a 500-apede.) In the past two Caras kids raised a mountain lion orphan for a zoo and handled other animal-related chores. A lot of formulas got mixed and a lot of messes cleaned up. At the time this book is being written our son, Clay, is a biology major and our daughter, Pamela, is engaged to be married to a zoo director. I am sure it is something in our blood. Most of our relatives think us peculiar—nice enough, but strange. We have never argued the point because I think we would lose.

Pamela began showing horses at ten. That was when Alexander joined us. He was and really still is a fine jumper who likes to fall down or duck into the bay whenever he has an inexperienced rider on his back. Sometimes he just runs away with them. Pamela learned early, the hard way, how to make a horse understand. I remember watching her return from a trail ride when she was about eleven. She was on foot and Alexander was walking behind her with his chin resting on her shoulder. I knew she had won a battle. She was mussed and dirty, but she and a thousand-pound horse had had it out and she had prevailed. In time, Star Billing and Orala joined the line-up, and before she left for college, Pamela had won over 350 ribbons and trophies. (I hope no one gives her any silver bowls or trays when she gets married. She has boxes full of them in the attic.)

Clay tried his hand and seat at riding and liked it well enough as a recreation, but the show ring was not for him. He had plenty of things to keep him busy, of course, with scuba diving and model building and his trail bike. Still, the idea of showing an animal other than a horse appealed to him. He approached his mother and me with the idea of a show dog of his own. We ran down the list and decided that none of the dogs we had on hand would stand a chance in serious competition. It had to be a new dog, a show-quality puppy. It was agreed I would pay for half and Clay, then fifteen, would pay for the other half from his earnings as an aide and kennel man at the local veterinary hospital. But what was the breed to be? One does have to pick the breed before one picks the dog.

We talked about the problem for several days, and all kinds of dogs came under consideration. It was generally agreed that it would be one of the smaller breeds. Clay was still in school in New York City, so for most of the year only part of each week could be spent at the country house. Whatever dog it was, since it was to be Clay's own special dog, it would not only have to spend part of the time in the apartment, but also would travel back and forth in a sedan or station wagon. Obviously it couldn't be a moose with a flea collar.

· 25 ·

The only thing we could achieve a consensus on was that it would be small. As for the rest of it—coat, temperament, working dog versus terrier, sporting dog versus non-sporting—all of it went back and forth in conversation, but no further than that.

Fortunately, the great annual event of dogdom was only a couple of weeks off. The Westminster Kennel Club Show was going to be staged at Madison Square Garden. One of the oldest uninterrupted sporting events in America (over a century, now), it brings together very nearly all the breeds and varieties recognized by the American Kennel Club. The number then stood at 135. Clearly, here was an unparalleled opportunity to see just about everything the world of dogs had to offer within a span of two days and evenings. It was decided that Clay would get his homework assignments in advance and spend from nine in the morning until eleven in the evening at the garden on the traditional Monday and Tuesday staging of the great show. (It was not exactly clear when he was going to do his homework, but he did take schoolbooks to Madison Square Garden with him.)

Before Clay set off for the first day of Westminster I urged him to take a long, careful look at Norwich terriers. They are a small animal, full of personality and much favored by people who have had an opportunity to know them. In England the breed is divided into two—Norwich (pronounced *norrich*) and Norfolk, depending on whether the ears stand up or flop over. In this country both kinds were then known as Norwich. Now we are following the English example.

I knew two people who owned Norwiches at the time. Peter Gimbel, an adventurer and filmmaker, and Carleton Ray, a marine biologist at Johns Hopkins. Since Peter has been engaged in some very hairy adventures with sharks and parachutes and Carleton has spent more time scuba diving under the Arctic and Antarctic ice packs than any other man in history, I was sure the Norwich must have real man-pleasing qualities. Although small, it is not a "sissy's" breed. I called both Peter and Carleton and received their assurance that this was a breed to please any outdoors-oriented boy. Clay went off to Madison

Square Garden with a special eye for the little ten-inch-high, eleven- to twelve-pound terrier.

After the Westminster show was over, Clay was noticeably silent about what if any decision he had come to. I decided not to press the point. Like all teenage boys, Clay had a time for thinking and a time for talking. I have always felt that is to be respected.

On Thursday of that week Clay approached me and somewhat hesitantly, I thought, said he had a breed in mind. Secure in the knowledge that one of the small terriers, if not the Norwich itself had won, I sat back to listen. Slowly, trying not to look either dumb or dumbstruck, I leaned forward in my chair.

"Bloodhound?"

Clay just looked at me. He knew it would take time to sink in. A full-grown bloodhound, a large male at least, can weigh almost as much as fourteen Norwich terriers, all packed into one burlap sack.

"Don't you think that is a little toward the other end of the scale?"

"They're nice dogs, Dad."

Once before, Clay had talked about this breed. Long before he let on he wanted to show a dog, he had gone to the Sportsmen's Show and spent time hanging around a display sponsored by the state police. The center of attraction in that display, I recalled, was a working bloodhound. He had talked about that dog for some time after.

It has to be obvious that anyone who lives in a house that is virtually a zoo has very little resistance and less common sense when it comes to adding animals to the Peaceable Kingdom. So, after resisting the idea of a bloodhound violently for nearly fifteen seconds, Jill, Clay, and I began pouring over a dozen dog books. As I recall, Clay discussed the matter with his sister long-distance later that night. Pamela, in the middle of preparing for a psychology exam, was diplomatically non-commital, acknowledging that the breed was *neat*. (Bloodhounds are distinctly not *neat*; they drool.)

Actually, I had attended Westminster, too. I was there filming a television report on the canine superbowl, and, although Clay and I had bumped into each other several times and had eaten a couple of Madison Square Garden hot dogs together, he had been on his own doing his research. One of the dogs I had used for my filmed report had been a great bloodhound male named Limbo, and, as I recalled, he was being attended or visited by a man with a turned-around collar. I wasn't sure whether he had been a Catholic or an Episcopalian priest, but one meets all kinds at dog shows. I also remembered that while I interviewed a former baseball star (we were sitting on a bench) a huge head had appeared between us and a great gaping maw had attempted to swallow the expensive microphone I was holding. It had been an amusing shot and we used it on the air. That had been a typical Limbo gambit.

I began checking. The man's name was Sinkinson, and it did not take long to determine that the kennel he and his wife owned produced the best bloodhounds in the country, including Limbo, the top-winning bloodhound in America at the time and for some years after. The next morning I checked with Jack Lafore, then president of the American Kennel Club, and Bob Taylor, then chairman of the Westminster Kennel Club Show.

"If you were buying a bloodhound for yourself where would you start?"

The answer was the same in both cases—Owings Mills, Maryland.

The first call I put through to the Sinkinsons left me a little shaken. Here I was, prepared to spend, in partnership with Clay, something like the annual budget of the U.S. Postal Service for a puppy (and not just incidentally offer it a great home) and they had treated me like a criminal!

Yes, they did have some very choice puppies, but no, I could not just buy one, not until I had been checked out to their satisfaction. Yes, they would meet with my wife, my son, and me, but no, they would not make a commitment. Yes, they would accept a deposit and hold a puppy, but I would have to be prepared to take the money back if any of us failed the IQ test or blood test or whatever else they chose to do to us. I began running down the list of things that they could possibly find wrong. I was a tad overweight, but that was offset by the fact that Clay's

· 28 ·

skin was clear. Our car was almost a year old, but Jill could always wear a pair of Gucci shoes. If Clay and I both got haircuts and we got the car waxed, perhaps there was a chance. I bought three breath-spray pocket gadgets and memorized several inoffensive jokes with church or pearly gate settings.

D-Day was a Saturday. We left New York early and drove the four hours to Owings Mills in a state of great apprehension. Clay did manage to fall asleep on the back seat, but Jill and I formed mental checklists over and over again. By the time we got to St. Thomas's Rectory, snuggling, as it does, in a small wooded valley of its own, we were quite uncertain whether or not we were good enough for a bloodhound. It was not the securest trip I have ever taken. What if we failed? How could we face each other? Can you imagine what the four-hour drive home would be like if we were told we weren't acceptable and were sent packing?

Speaking for myself, at least, I was absolutely shaky when we turned into the long, curving drive. By the time we had passed the second BLOODHOUND CROSSING sign with its splendid silhouette of a magnificent hound, I was ready to turn around and head for home. Why run the risk of finding out you are a total failure? Why should buying a puppy for cash money be a two-Valium deal? The thought that there were 134 other breeds and varieties to choose from didn't help. But it was too late to turn back; we were there. The drive was narrow. At the very least we would have had to pull into their backyard, swing a U-turn, and make a run for it. Clay was for pressing on.

Jackie and Sink were waiting for us as we pulled up and parked behind their "rig," as they called their dog-show-going camper bus. Wouldn't you know! There was post-ignition and the car spluttered to a noisy stop. On the hillside a dozen huge hounds ululated and the Maryland countryside rang with the greeting only these hounds are capable of producing. Chins to the sky, they roll out notes Beethoven would have heard (and copied). No less than poodle fanciers admit that bloodhounds have a sound about them. Even if you don't like the look, that sound summons up memories that go back to the cave.

To our relief, and my enduring gratitude, Jackie and Sink were delightful. I had half expected to put one foot out of the car only to have them scream at me to get back in and leave at once. But no, we were greeted warmly and asked would we care for some refreshments or would we like to see some of their dogs first? We opted for dogs.

All of the excitement that The Rectory dogs engender whenever they appear in public was understandable as we met R. J. (Yankee's father), Rebby, and the rest of the pack. Here were dogs you could thump. (Did you ever notice that people thump big dogs? Perhaps it is the bass drum sound their rib cages make, but people thump rather than pet them.) As each dog was brought out it licked and squirmed and displayed its incomparable hound charm. It was not difficult to understand what it was that had appealed to Clay. It was then that we first met Yankee. He was just under six months old and leggy, but he had a head like a statue. His coat was pure satin and his ears looked like vertical scatter rugs. Somehow the idea got through to us that if we all passed both the written and oral exams, and the physical examination, he might be made available under certain terms. I recall thinking at the time how much easier Clay had been to come by than Clay's dog.

Actually, what the Sinkinsons were doing was what all really fine breeders do. They were assuring themselves that their dog was going to a suitable home. They wanted the dog to be really well cared for as well as loved, and handled by fine professional handlers. They wanted their dog to be seen to advantage and *finished,* that is, campaigned or shown until the coveted Ch. (meaning *champion*) appeared in front of his name.

It was then time for refreshments. Leaving Clay outside to bask in a glory of hounds, we four adults went inside. What followed was easy conversation. Apparently, the checking on them I had done before calling was at least equaled by the checking on us they had done after my call. We all seemed to know a bit about each other, and that wasn't really unpleasant. Their caution wasn't based on suspicion but on the desire for goodwill and success.

Eventually Clay came in and we sat around a table of crystal, silver, and bone china and were served a splendid roast beef dinner. That was really my one big goof of the day. I thought that I had surely blown it when I hit the beef before grace was said. It was not a ritual with which I was particularly familiar. I knew about it, of course, from watching "The Waltons" on television, but I hadn't anticipated it. Later, upon reflection, that was pretty dumb. Sink shot me a look and smiled a nice "you're going to love it in hell" smile and we all bowed our heads. I am afraid I prayed for approval, acceptance, some sign, earthly or heavenly that the Caras's were in.

The Sinkinson rules for the dogs they released were understandable when you realized what went into producing puppies like Yankee. Some of the clauses in the contract we signed specified:

1. The puppy could never be sold without offering the Sinkinsons an opportunity to buy it back first.

2. The puppy would be shown until it had achieved champion status.

3. Twelve-inch-high stands for food and water dishes would be provided. It is not good for a bloodhound's posture (or the posture of any very large dog) to lean its head to the ground for eating and drinking. Considering the number of hours a bloodhound spends with its nose to the ground while interpreting its world or following a trail, I have never quite understood that stipulation.

4. The puppy's nails would be cut twice a week so that his feet would knuckle up and be both comfortable and nice to look at. Long nails are terrible for dogs. This ritual continues for as long as the dog lives, and bloodhounds like having their nails cut as much as we like paying income tax. It is an ugly, evil fact of life. It doesn't hurt when done properly, but every bloodhound is sure it looks like something that has to hurt, or should hurt, or will hurt someday.

5. We would follow the diet regimen suggested by the Sinkinsons and provided on a printed sheet. Jackie was quite willing to call our veterinarian and explain to him what he had failed to learn in veterinary school. (Subsequently this is exactly what happened. Our vet admits to this day that he learned a great deal from her.) Diet is terribly important in building a fine show dog, but it has an even more critical meaning. All deep-chested dogs like bloodhounds are susceptible to a deadly condi-

tion called bloat. A build-up of gas and a form of spasm or tortion can put a large dog into shock and kill it in less than an hour. It is avoided, in part, by feeding an adult dog at least twice a day. Two smaller meals are safer than one big one.

6. The dog would be exercised on soft surfaces. Hard surfaces like concrete and tar are bad for a heavy dog's feet. It makes them break down in the pastern, an area on the leg also known as the metacarpus. It comes between the wrist, or *carpus,* and the *digits,* or toes. (These are words all of us bloodhound people know. We say things like that all the time. Anyone who can say pastern without looking around to see if a good impression is being made has been on the inside for at least several hours.)

There were lots of other stipulations, too, but the most important one was that we were about to get both a bloodhound puppy and a mother-in-law, or the canine-world equivalent of that noble sort. Jackie was to be on the phone with Jill all the time. If the poor woman does that for all her puppies, one wonders when she sleeps or does other things that can't possibly allow for a phone to the ear. In short, we would buy Yankee and the Sinkinsons would adopt us. No wonder they had been noncommittal. We were about to become family, and I didn't even know about saying grace!

Five

Within an hour of coffee and brandy, in a very mellow room full of mellow people, the deal was made. I would sell a couple of cars, part of our art collection, take a second job nights, and Yankee would be ours. It was a nice feeling and Jill, Clay, and I vaguely suspected, we later confessed to one another, that something grand was about to start.

There was some contract signing, some more advice and explanations and we started home. Yankee, perfectly happy as he is to this day with any empathetic human being, stretched out on the back seat with his head on Clay's lap and began to snore. We stopped often and let him have a sniff at a bit of grass. At one stop I was walking Yankee while Clay and Jill popped into the rest stop when a van pulled up. It had Georgia plates. A young man stuck his head out the window and whistled.

"Hey, mister, that's some kind of a hound dawg you got there."

I waved in appreciation and the van pulled away. That particular greeting had special meanings. It is in the Deep South that hounds are really appreciated. Up north they are very much less known. That kind of unsolicited approval from a Georgian bode well for the future. Yankee was indeed *some kind of hound dawg.*

We finally reached the city apartment, and Yankee did a slow, careful circuit checking out smells. On his own he found Clay's room and curled up on a rug beside the bed. He knew instinctively to whom he belonged. Bloodhounds, like all dogs I would give house room to, love kids. No one can ever convince me a dog cannot judge the age of the people with whom it comes in contact.

Yankee was not housebroken. As a kennel dog that had not been an issue, but in a house and an apartment it was a big one. He didn't lift his leg yet, but he could float the tile right off the floor, or crush it. Frequent walks were absolutely necessary, and a routine was established: out six times every day, and no less than three very long blocks each time. At least three walks would be a mile or more in length. That wouldn't be a problem at the house, where there was plenty of land right out the back door, but in the city it had to come down to a system.

It took Yankee about thirty-six hours to figure out that he still had to go, just as he had in Maryland, but there were places that made us happy and places that made him sad. Any sign of disapproval makes a bloodhound very sad, indeed. They hate to be yelled at and scolded and they love to be praised. They are, in fact, despite their size, the world's biggest sops.

Four days after Yankee arrived in New York City we had Bob Taylor to dinner. Bob and his wife Jane are two of the most delightful, knowledgeable, and decorative figures in the dog world. Bob had been one of the two people who had turned us to Maryland when Clay had first brought up the subject of a man-trailing hound. Jane was out of town, but Bob came to dinner to see what his advice had wrought. He examined Yankee knowingly and agreed that we had come by a terrific dog, one that could go all the way and make a name for himself. Clay was glowing. Bob was sitting there with a drink in his hand. I was boasting about how easy it had been to housebreak Yankee.

"How long did it take you to housebreak him?" Bob asked.

"Less than two days," I answered with obvious gasconade.

"Then why is he peeing in my shoe?"

Yankee was! Even as I boasted of his good manners he was squatting over Bob Taylor's foot wearing a benign expression on his face.

"I hate to think what he would do to me if I were a judge," Bob remarked—unfeelingly, I thought.

Clay rushed Yankee off to the elevator and down the seven floors to the street. I don't know what they talked about on the way out, but I can guess. Jill and I paraded back from the kitchen trailing streamers of

· 34 ·

paper towels. As Bob tried to fend off the paper assault by assuring us that his foot would dry, someday, we dabbed and spluttered. It was a real bloodhound moment. Why there? Why then? No one knows but Yankee, and he has never talked about it.

The weekend came, and it was time for the country house. Yankee had already shown us on the trip up from Maryland that he was a good traveler, something that is absolutely essential for a show dog, and the trip out was full of the same snores and sighs. At the house Yankee met his first cats. He thought that they were wonderful inventions. They could be pinned with a single paw, they made outrageous noises and they smelled interesting if not terrific.

There were also other dogs. Pudge, the bulldog, was a bitch, and she was great to butt and chase. Jeremy was a large male golden retriever, but a very peaceful fellow by nature, so there was no conflict there. Ludo, the ancient male Yorkshire terrier, was just plain sick and tired of seeing new animals come into his world and wanted to be left alone. That made him fun to tease. Oomiac, the Siberian husky bitch, was pleasant, and Nel Gwinn, the random-bred bitch, was too old and venerable not to respect. And there were two other sympathetic people, too. My in-laws, Jim and Phyllis Barclay, were in permanent residence. It was a good household, Yankee concluded, and he settled right in with enthusiasm. In the Caras version of the Peaceable Kingdom that kind of adaptability on the part of each animal is essential. As he took his first nap in his new country home Yankee was bathed by two cats scandalized by his doggy odor. It would take a lot of time before they realized that horses smell like horses, cows like cows, and bloodhounds very much like dogs, permanently.

There were, in fact, no problems at all. Yankee had visited both his homes—which would be his homes for life. He liked both, liked the human members of the family and the animal ones as well. Because he was to spend his life in a fairly active household, all of that was terribly important. A lot of people pass through the Caras zoo in the course of the year; and a couple of times a year, on the average, parties get out of hand and anywhere from seventy to ninety people may descend during a single afternoon and evening. There are a lot of weekend guests, too, and some of them bring animals with them. A very large dog that was uptight about strange animals or, even worse, strange people, would be just about impossible to contend with. A dog of the size Yankee would grow to be is head/face/throat high on a child; and jaws long enough to form that great muzzle are too powerful to joke about. A nervous or ill-tempered dog would have to shape up or ship out. It never was to become an issue. From the moment we first met him, Yankee thought every creature on this green planet was lovely.* Everything is worth at least a tail wag, and most things a good nuzzle. Although Yankee was never a kisser, he is one to poke you with his nose or lay it on your knee. Yankee had, even then at the beginning, one of the nicest attitudes toward life I have ever encountered in man or animal. He really believes in loving his neighbor. It has almost always paid off. The one great exception was my pet albino corn snake. I was cleaning his cage in my study and Clay was holding the little pink-eyed beast when Yankee came up for a sniff. After all, a snake is an interesting new smell. The corn snake nailed Yankee right on the nose and made it bleed. Yankee said "Oooof" and sat down hard. He has avoided snakes ever since.

---

*Actually, not every creature. For some reason, Yankee has always taken exception to standard poodles in show clip. Every time he sees one he sets up a terrible fuss. There is something about the look that seems to challenge him.

Six

Since Yankee was six months old, it was time to start his show career. Puppies are started at that age. Although they may not set the show world on its ear at first, it is a learning process for the dog, an opportunity for the handler to get to know his or her charge, and a very important chance for owners to learn how to deal with a knotted stomach.

Before going on to tell how Yankee became a champion, it is important to be sure we all understand how a dog show works. Actually, *works* is not the best word because it doesn't work so much as it *happens.* A dog show occurs, as does an accident, bringing its tears and leaving its scars. A dog show is an incident, an occasion, always an event. No one is exactly sure how it all comes together, but it does.

The lowest event in a dog show is called a *class* and it is full of, not all that surprisingly, class dogs. There are Puppy Classes—one for males (dogs) and one for females (bitches). Any contestant between the ages of six months and one year may be entered as a puppy. The same dog or bitch may be shown in Open Class, which is literally open to just about any class dog or bitch. (At this level there are separate classes for males and females.) Besides Open and Puppy there are American Bred, Bred by Owner, and one or two other classes. The entries in these classes have not yet won their championship. They are dogs on the rise. At six months, Yankee was certainly that.

All classes, of course, are limited to one single breed and sometimes to one variety of a breed. You will not find a class Doberman pinscher competing with a class corgi. So there you have all of the male bloodhounds at the show that day over six months old and under twelve months old facing off in the male Puppy Class—except those that are in that age group that are being shown as Open dogs and also excepting any male bloodhound wonder dogs who are already champions—and we'll get to them in a minute.

The male puppy that wins his class must then face all the other male dogs that win their classes in that same breed that day. The best Puppy dog versus the best Open dog versus the best American Bred dog, and so on.

The class dog that beats all the other class dogs and the class bitch that beats all the other class bitches earn points. They are known as Winner's Dog and Winner's Bitch. The points thus earned go toward their championship status. How many points does it take to become a champion? Fifteen, but that fifteen includes two "majors": that is, show wins where three or more points are awarded, *and* the two major wins must be under two different judges. Getting your "majors" can be the most trying problem in campaigning a dog. Many dogs keep winning two-point shows after they get their first major and build up many more than their fifteen points without being designated a champion. The second major can be slow in coming.

How many points does a class dog get when it goes Winner's Bitch or Winner's Dog? It depends. There is a sliding scale, and it varies in different parts of the country. What it depends on is the popularity of the breed and how many dogs are entered in the show on a given day. A poodle has to beat many more dogs than a bloodhound does to earn points or win a major. Poodles rank first in popularity in this country and bloodhounds rank fifty-fifth.

Anyway, once a dog and a bitch have been designated Winner's Dog and Winner's Bitch they enter Best-of-Breed competition. They are in the ring with all the champions of record of their breed who are entered that day. It is not very often that a class dog beats the champions, but—as we'll see—that can happen. In this Best-of-Breed competition the judge picks Best-of-Winners from between the Winner's Dog and the Winner's Bitch. It isn't as good as Best-of-Breed, but it's better than a poke in the eye with a sharp stick.

Once the Best-of-Breed is selected, the going gets tough. That dog or bitch will then represent its breed in *group competition.* There are no points beyond the Best-of-Winners level. That is, you don't get points for Best-of-Breed or higher, but the honors above that level are terribly important to a dog's, an owner's, and a handler's reputations.

There are six groups (I hope you are still with me!): Hound, Terrier, Sporting, Working, Toy, and Non-Sporting. All dogs eligible to earn points at a show are in one of these groups, as are all dogs eligible to compete for Best-in-Show.

Late in the afternoon the group competitions begin. The classes are all over, new champions established, and many dogs are on their way home. Now, in each group the Best-of-Breed dog or bitch for each breed in the group enters the ring. In the Hound Group, for example, besides a bloodhound you will see one each of the following: Afghan, basenji, basset, beagle, black and tan coonhound, borzoi, dachshund, American foxhound, English foxhound, greyhound, harrier, Irish wolfhound, Norwegian elkhound, otter hound, Rhodesian ridgeback, saluki, Scottish deerhound, and whippet, each the winner of a Best-of-Breed ribbon that day.

There can be some confusion in names. The Italian greyhound will not be in the ring; it is in the Toy Group. Nor will the Keeshond be in with the Hound Group; it belongs in Non-Sporting. However, people who show dogs get used to that kind of thing. You just ignore them and pretend you understand everything that is going on. Everyone else is pretending, so why shouldn't you? The trick is to look all-knowing, sophisticated, or above it all. If it gets out of hand and you are hopelessly bewildered, you can always slump down into a canvas chair and sob. People will think it's an allergy to dogs.

All right, then, the judge now has all of the Best-of-Breed hounds in the Hound Group. How do you judge a dachshund against a bloodhound? That is like a goldfish versus a great white shark! You don't, or more correctly, the judge doesn't. Any judge who knows enough to be a group judge presumably knows the standards of each of the breeds in that group. He or she judges each dog against the standards for its own breed. The bloodhound is viewed against the theoretical bloodhound standard of perfection and the dachshund against its standard, and so on down the line.

Eventually the group dogs are selected down to four—the four most perfect examples in the group that day. There is a Group I winner, which is a very high honor. There are also placements for Group II, Group III, and Group IV. Any of the four titles adds greatly to a dog's or bitch's luster and reputation, but only the Group I or Group Winner goes on to further competition that day. At this point, of course, from the time the Best-of-Breed competition starts, segregation of the sexes is out. Dogs and bitches are all shown together. Only on the class level are they apart.

In the final event of the day the Group Winners from each of the six groups are shown together. The Best-in-Show judge also judges the dogs in the ring against their own standards, not directly against each other. One dog or bitch is chosen Best-in-Show and that animal's stock soars. Its owner gives the handler a great big bonus, sometimes gets drunk and runs up a terrible phone bill in the motel that night. It is very exciting. Even when you don't know what is going on there is an infectious excitement and everybody shares in a series of common experiences: sore feet, aching calves, indigestion from ferocious frankfurters that apparently object to being eaten, too much beer or soda, wrinkled clothes, petty politics, and gossip. It is a great happening and it all costs money. The people who get caught up in it often explain to their psychiatrists that they couldn't live without it. It is addictive. Psychiatrists love such patients. They know they never will be well.

And so, according to the terms of the Caras-Sinkinson Treaty, Yankee's time had come. We were committed to seeing him through all the way to his championship. Everyone who saw him agreed he had the potential to make it.

His first show was etched into history on April 26, 1975. I was away and Clay was in school. Suddenly Jill was on her own. It had been decided that Jackie would show Yankee at the beginning, not only because she is one of the best bloodhound handlers that has ever lived, but because she has fixed ideas about how a young dog of this sensitive breed should be broken in. She needn't have worried. Yankee loved the whole thing. He didn't break in, the world did.

The first show was in Stanton, Delaware, and was being staged by the Wilmington Kennel Club. Jill was to drive down the evening before and meet Jackie there. She set out in good faith and on the New Jersey Turnpike found roughly the equivalent of Lake Superior falling onto the station wagon from above. It was a true cloudburst and it got the car's wires wet, or something, and the engine conked out. She sat there until the storm passed and eventually got the car started again. When she and Yankee, who had slept through the entire turnpike trauma, reached the motel it was raining again. The room they were assigned was on the second floor and accessible only by an outside metal staircase. Yankee took one look at the metal stairs and snorted. Not him! He sat down and yawned.

Jill plunked her purse and suitcase back in the wagon and carried the seventy-pound Yankee up the metal stairs, barely maintaining her footing. She locked him in the room and went back down for her bag, her purse, his food, feeding stand, and metal dishes. (He is allergic to plastic dishes. They make his nose go all pink and nasty looking.) In the time it took her to get all of that up the stairs (still in the rain) and into the room, Yankee had eaten much of the bedspread. Something had made him nervous, and that made Jill nervous. That night, while thunder and lightning shook the motel, Jill and Yankee cuddled in one bed reassuring each other that dawn would be different and they would live to see it. Jill was having a proper indoctrination into the world of dog shows.

The next morning, at Delaware Park, Jill rendezvoused with Jackie and was told not to expect anything very impressive that first time out. Yankee would be nervous and unhappy and would not show well. It was the experience that counted.

Jackie was wrong. Yankee loved it. He thought the other dogs were lovely and that the judge, Mrs. M. Lynwood Walton, was grand. He liked the smells and the noise and reacted to the confusion as if it were something he had caused himself for a lark. Mrs. Walton liked Yankee, too, and his charm won out. He was quickly tagged Best Puppy Dog, his first ribbon. When Winner's Dog and Winner's Bitch are chosen there is a Reserve Winner chosen for each, just in case either is later disqualified. Jill felt it was too much to hope that Yankee would get Winner's Dog in his first show. She was right, but as further recognition he went Reserve Winner. Two ribbons the first time out, although, of course, no points. That didn't matter. Yankee was a born show dog; he loved it, he was cool, and the judges and crowds liked him. Later, when there would be applause, he would show just how much he loved the whole mad scene.

Seven

There is often some confusion as to exactly what a *handler* is or what a handler does. A handler is the person who physically puts a dog through its paces in the ring. It is the responsibility of the handler to present the dog to the judge in a way that will accentuate all of its strong points and mask, insofar as that is possible, its faults.

A judge is looking for the dog's skeletal structure. The judge wants to know how that dog is put together. Top-line (the back line once the dog is set up in approved show dog stance), rib cage, legs, tail set, all of these things are best viewed in two modes, when the dog is set up and when the dog is moving. Putting a dog through the regimen in the ring so that it always looks its best is not easy. When done well, it attests to years of experience. Professional handlers usually charge between thirty and fifty dollars per show. There are extra charges if the dog places in its group or goes Best-in-Show. Traditionally, owners allow handlers to keep any cash awards for those high wins.

Handlers, of course, can be no better than the dogs they handle. They want fine dogs not only because it means another fee but because when a dog is obviously going on to big wins they want to be the handler whose picture gets taken with the judge, the dog, and the trophy. The difference between the best-known handlers in America and the least-known, obviously, can be measured in the wins they have achieved—that is, the quality of the dogs they have handled. An owner has a tough time getting a fine handler for a mediocre dog, and the owner of a fine dog has no trouble at all. Fortunately, in his time, Yankee would enter the ring with some of the best.

There is another factor in all of this, although people don't often like to talk about it. Owners want top handlers even if their fees may be a little higher. Many handlers are so experienced and so very well known that some judges—well, if they don't fear them, they at least pay them a lot of attention. "Here comes Brutus V. Buddenbrook with a new komondor," they think. "He wouldn't touch a new komondor unless it had something. I had better take a long careful look." There is no doubt that many judges are to some degree influenced to look harder than usual when a star handler marches a new dog into the ring. It is not different from a lot of other things in life. You will certainly judge a television show, movie, or play on its own merits, but you will be more likely to watch that event if a top star is in it. It is the same thing when a star handler appears. One can anticipate, at least, the possibility of a star dog.

Yankee's second show was during a ferocious heat wave late in May in Monmouth, New Jersey. There was a puppy sweepstakes and Yankee took second place and won $5.40. That covered the highway tolls to and from the show, almost. In Puppy Class, Yankee again won the blue ribbon, just as he had at Delaware. He got a nice pewter trophy from Judge William L. Barton. But again, of course, no points.

We learned an unpleasant side of some dog show people that day. It was broiling hot and there wasn't a cloud in the sky. Some people locked their dogs in their cars and headed for the beer concession, under a broad tent. The loudspeaker kept on blaring warnings that dogs were in trouble in locked cars. All dogs should be removed from closed cars at once. Still, some people; conspicuous without a dog at their side, stayed in the shade of the beer concession tent. The state police, making the rounds of the parking lot, found a bulldog unconscious in a closed and locked car. They broke into the car and administered oxygen. The dog, we were told, later died. And still the loudspeaker repeated the warnings over and over again. *There is a Plymouth wagon with two borzois in trouble. There is a Doberman in trouble in a Cadillac at the west end of the parking lot.*

Finally, a young man took matters into his own hands. He went over to the announcer's table, grabbed the microphone, and announced that he was going into the parking lot with a jack handle. He was going to smash the windshield on any car with a dog locked inside. The beer tent emptied in a hurry.

What we had learned, of course, was what we had always suspected. Not all people who own or show dogs love dogs, or even like them. Such people are in a minority. To them dogs are just possessions to sire and bear puppies which can be sold. The dogs themselves mean nothing. In our experience people like that are perhaps no more than five percent of the whole. Still, we see them and avoid them. We have never found a bloodhound owner in that category, happy to say.

Two days after Monmouth, there was another show in Rockaway Park, New York. Again Yankee was entered, although Jackie couldn't be there. A young friend of ours named Kristin Killilea handled Yankee most expertly. The combination of teenage girl and adolescent puppy did it, and in his third straight show Yankee took his third first-place ribbon in his class. No points, but a clear indication that he wasn't too shoddy a dog.

Throughout it all Yankee showed the same enthusiasm. He thought the noise and confusion and smells were wonderful. He liked the judging because it meant that hands got rubbed all over him to feel out his substance and skeleton. The handler, of course, paid him a great deal of attention and he was praised highly for being a good boy in the ring when it was over. From the day of his first show until now Yankee has always looked on showing as a positive experience.

In July of 1975 Kristin showed Yankee again, at Wading River, New York. He was the only bloodhound being shown, so he took Puppy Class, Best-of-Winners, and Winner's Dog and Best-of-Breed as well. He got the ribbons, but, obviously, with no competition, there were no points. However, the judge did not have to award the ribbons if he felt the dog being shown was unworthy. Yankee was worthy and was gaining in experience. Each time he went into the ring he looked better and set up and moved with more assurance and grace. Experience helps even with things that come naturally.

It happened in Maine, in August. Yankee was launched. At the Central Maine Kennel Club show in Gorham, not far from Portland, Judge Len Carey gave Yankee the Puppy Class, Winner's Dog, and Best-of-Winners. He had his first two points—thirteen to go, including those two majors.

The very next day, on the same show grounds in Gorham, the Penobscot Valley Kennel Club held its show. Mrs. W. P. Wear gave Yankee his class, Winner's Dog, and, amid screams and shouts, Best-of-Breed. One of the champions he beat that day was the mighty Limbo, the top-winning bloodhound in America at the time. Yankee had two more points—a total of four for two days. The shout went up: "The puppy did it! The puppy did it!" Yankee sat back on his haunches and yodeled. The crowd loved it, and so did the Carases. It really is very exciting. It even beats bingo.

There was a third show in the area the next day. The Vacationland Dog Club had its annual event. The judge, Mrs. Winifred L. Heckman, again gave Yankee his class and Best-of-Winners. That meant another two points. In three days of real campaigning Yankee went almost halfway. There never had been any doubts about him; but if there had been, they would have been dispelled on August 31, 1975. Yankee was born to win, and no one knew that better than he did. You cannot spend much time around a show dog and not believe the dogs know what they are doing. It is in their very soul. As long as they get the loving care they need, they will work their hearts out to show well in the ring.

There were two other shows early in September when Yankee took his class and Reserve Winner both times, but without points. Things really began rolling again on September 28. In Westbury, New York, under Judge William W. Brainard, Jr., Yankee went to Best-of-Winners in what proved to be a three-point major. Not only had he passed the halfway mark with his total of nine points, he had satisfied half his major requirements. People began recognizing him when he appeared at shows. They came up to talk to us about things in general, and about Yankee. In October he took three more points in two shows. He was up to twelve. One more three-point major would do it all.

On November 30 he took two more points in Atlantic City, fourteen out of his fifteen points, but still that second major eluded us. It all came together on December 6 at the Kennel Club of Philadelphia. At the age of thirteen months, under Judge Alice Bartlett Lane, Yankee took his second and last major, earned three more points for a total of seventeen, and became Champion The Rectory's Yankee Patriot. He would bear that title for life, nothing could take it away from him. In a total of fourteen shows, including the early puppy learning shows, he had become a Champion. Further, he had never entered into a show when he did not win his class.

Throughout all his showing, Yankee introduced us to a wide variety of people. People who did not know us would walk up and start talking to Yankee. Out of politeness they would get around to us, and we made some very nice friends.

I am sure it is the same with all the other breeds, but there is a kind of camaraderie among bloodhound owners. They have a number of things in common: spit on their clothing (also called slop, slobber, and drool) and one arm longer than the other. All of that plus the great slobber-chops themselves. I don't think that anyone who has not owned one of these dogs can appreciate what all of this means, besides the fact that bloodhound owners are a little crazy. That surmise is accurate, of course, but there is that other thing. Bloodhound people like to think that they are to other dog owners what the person who follows the score at a symphonic performance is to the run-of-the-mill music listener. They operate on a plane other people just can't be expected to understand. Perhaps that is true, and perhaps it is not. What counts is that bloodhound owners feel that way, and their dogs agree. It is a great racket for the dogs. They get treated like royalty.

Eight

We always knew there would be another side to owning a bloodhound. Besides being just another beautiful face, Yankee was a million-dollar nose on the hoof. He was, after all, a trailing dog.

When my interest in bloodhounds first began to blossom as a result of Clay's confusing them with little terriers I was involved in a survey of the tragic New York City zoos, not to be confused with the superb Bronx Zoo also in New York. I was working on the city-run zoos. I was employed by a private foundation to do a study, although, for a myriad of reasons, all tied up with New York City's political wonderland (or, should we say, no-man's-land), the job could not be done. Anyway, it occurred to some city officials that if Caras knew enough about lions and tigers to consult with zoo people, he must know about bloodhounds, too. It was strictly a fortuitous coincidence.

It was decided a test would be run using New York City detectives as targets and a New York State Police bloodhound as a targeteer. On a bright and brisk fall morning our corps of observers stood on the roof of the Central Park Precinct house and directed operations with walkie-talkies. There seemed to be enough police brass on the roof to sink the ancient stone building. Kojak would have loved it.

Two detectives were sent out into the park and told to walk side-by-side. At a given point one detective was ordered to drop his jacket and split off from his companion. He now would become the hound's target.

The target-detective was directed to walk a random but roughly zigzag course across an area of Central Park known as the Sheep Meadow. The evening before there had been a rock concert in the meadow attended by 55,000 people. To a bloodhound, each of those 55,000 trails was still alive. A detective walking through the middle would be just one more trail added to the total.

After the Sheep Meadow was behind him, the detective, on instructions from the brass on the roof, was directed through an area where no fewer than nine softball games were in progress and from there through an area where about a dozen people were walking their dogs. It was a park ramble near the police station where elderly people felt safe to walk, sit, and take the sun. They often brought their dogs along.

Once the detective had passed the second area, the softball games-in-progress, the state trooper was told to pick up the trail. He took his great hound from the back of his truck and slipped a harness over its head and fastened it around its barrel chest. That meant, to the hound, that it was about to go to work. The trooper spotted the jacket on the ground in the area where he had been advised to work and took his bloodhound over to it. When they were standing over the garment, the trooper took the long heavy leather lead from the dog's collar and snapped it onto the D-ring on the harness. At the same time he dropped the dog's nose to the jacket and gave the two-word command that dominates a trailing bloodhound's life: "Find 'em."

Once the lead is attached to the harness and tugged to let the dog know it is there and once that command is given, the hound takes a couple of good, deep breaths and that is it. He will not stop until he finds the source of that smell or hopelessly loses it through no fault of his own. It is like turning on a computer. The smell is etched onto the dog's brain.

The state police bloodhound took off with a tug. The trail was only minutes old, which to him meant burning hot. (The record age for a trail run successfully by a bloodhound is believed to have been 104 hours old.) The Sheep Meadow with its 55,001 trails offered no problem. The great dog moved off, following the detective's course exactly. The ball games, too, meant nothing. The dog never even looked up. The other dogs being walked? It was as if they weren't there. Within five minutes of being told to "find 'em" the dog stood beside the unbelieving detective, panting and waiting for his reward.

"Sure!" the police officials acknowledged. "On grass. But how about on city streets?"

The state trooper was told by radio to divert his dog while the city detective left the park and headed out onto Fifth Avenue. He was then directed into one of the busy transverses that cross the park and from there into the courtyard behind the precinct house. He was told to cut through a motorbike and police car repair shop filled with grease, oil, exhaust, and other hydrocarbons that supposedly will destroy a dog's scenting ability for hours. From there he was sent across a cobblestone courtyard where two hundred uniformed officers had been mustered for roll call that morning and from there into an office building. Five minutes later the great bloodhound stood beside him, drooling onto his knee.

The New York City police were terribly impressed, but since they had gone on record as having said that what they had just seen wasn't possible, they decided not to add bloodhounds to the police force. No one in government likes to acknowledge even the possibility of error or misjudgment. The results of that morning's tests could be buried. It is easy to shuffle reports. They never have to get circulated. The original reluctance of police to engage hounds would be a little more difficult to erase from the record.

It was the results of that test, not New York City police brass rank-closing, that were on my mind as Clay, Yankee, and I headed north for Schodack, New York. The Police Bloodhound Association was having its annual meeting and had been nice enough to invite a boy and his hound to join in. I was going as chaperone and filmmaker.

The small community of Schodack was no place to commit a crime that weekend. It swarmed with FBI agents, bounty hunters, state troopers, detectives, and city and town police officers from all over the country. They had all come bringing their man-trailing hounds with them. This was their annual opportunity to put the dogs through their paces under the watchful eyes of the most experienced trailing men in

Rebby (Champion The Rectory's Rebel Yell) with her litter. One of those puppies is Yankee. Bloodhound puppies are black at birth. *The Rev. George Sinkinson*

Yankee (second from the left) and his littermates behind the rectory house. *The Rev. George Sinkinson*

Clay and Yankee the first time they met. Yankee was then six months and Clay fifteen years old. *R. Caras*

"R. J." (Champion The Rectory's Wisdom), Yankee's father. *The Rev. George Sinkinson*

Amanda Blake (*Gunsmoke*'s Miss Kitty) with Yankee in the Caras backyard. *R. Caras*

A head shot of Yankee by the world's greatest dog photographer, Alton Anderson.

Cartoonist Charles Addams with two of Yankee's offspring: Penny is on the right and Digger (Champion The Rectory's Prodigal Son) on the left. *R. Caras*

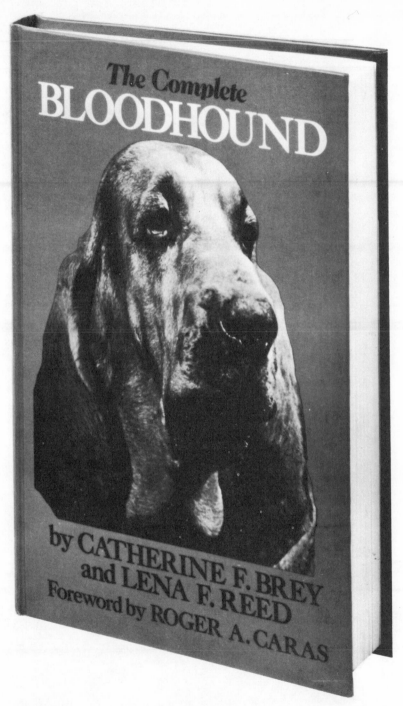

The Complete
BLOODHOUND

by CATHERINE F. BREY
and LENA F. REED
Foreword by ROGER A. CARAS

Yankee as a cover boy: Howell Book House's long-awaited blood-hound breed book. The picture used was taken by Alton Anderson. *Courtesy, Howell Book House, Inc., publisher of* THE COMPLETE BLOODHOUND

Waiting to go into the ring. A pensive moment at Madison Square Garden captured by photographer Shana Sureck.

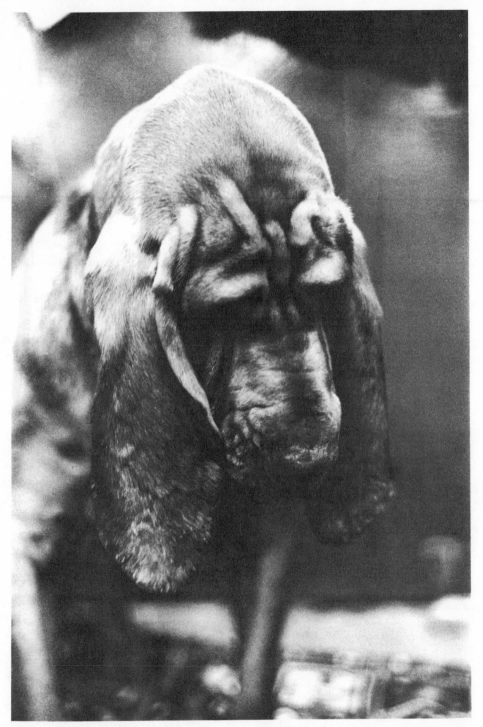

When you lose you have to think about it. Another moment recorded by Ms. Sureck.

Jackie Sinkinson with Yankee's magnificent son Digger. Tragically he would die of a mysterious infection before he was three. *Bill Gilbert*

The author with Penny, left, and Yankee, right. *Bill Gilbert*

Yankee by Alton Anderson, one of scores of studies done by the great photographer.

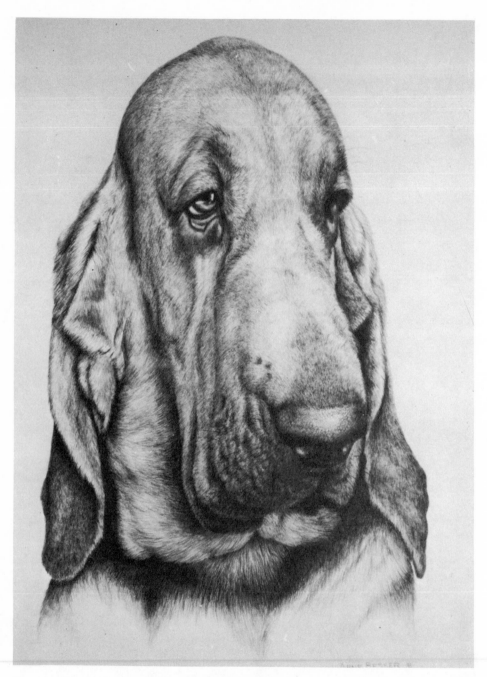

Pencil study of Yankee by the artist Arne Besser. Seven different kinds of pencils were used to get the tones and shades. *Clay Caras*

Study of Penny by the artist Rod Arbogast. *Clay Caras*

Yankee by the artist Mike
Landi. *Clay Caras*

Bronze sculpture of Penny by the artist and great dog handler Damra Bolte. *Clay Caras*

A naïve painting of Yankee by the artist Anne Stanwell. *Clay Caras*

Yankee as Charles de Gaulle, envisioned in a painting and collage by the artist Pol. *Clay Caras*

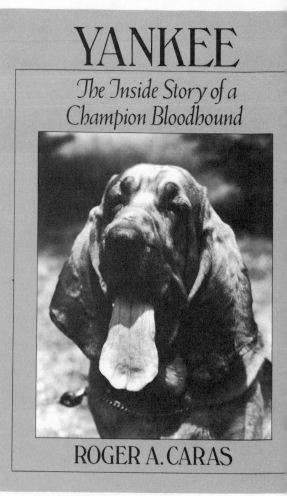

YANKEE

The Inside Story of a Champion Bloodhound

ROGER A. CARAS

Yankee, star and champion, once again a cover boy. *Alton Anderson*

Sketch of a Yankee mood by Bill Dehn.
Clay Caras

the country. These were the people who routinely recovered lost children, hikers, and mental patients, and occasionally escaped convicts. It was their hobby as well as their job and many of the men, FBI agents included, ran the dogs as just that—a hobby—when they were off duty. They gave their services and those of their dogs free to their communities. A few of the men were bounty hunters from southern states. They got paid twenty-five dollars for each escaped convict they recaptured. We arrived to find a colorful bunch of men (and a few women) and a swirling mass of huge, excited, and therefore noisy dogs. Clay and Yankee both looked absolutely bewildered. I tried to look calm, cool, and collected. What I really wanted to do was hide behind Clay and Yankee.

The four-day seminar included lectures by lawyers from district attorneys' offices on how to prepare evidence gathered by bloodhounds, the recounting of recent important "finds" by some of the dogs present, and field work. In the field each person-and-dog combination was assigned to an expert. There were green dogs like Yankee with no experience at all, semi-experienced dogs that needed some fine detail work, and old hounds that had picked up bad habits like preferring deer trailing to man trailing. Clay and Yankee were assigned a police officer named Jim Zarifis, who, by fortunate coincidence, came from our part of Long Island. Since the only youngsters supposed to be involved were children of law enforcement officers, an FBI agent volunteered to adopt Clay for a few days. Clay seemed to like the idea very much.

Clay managed to borrow a harness, and at the right moment a nice ripe T-shirt was shoved under Yankee's nose. "Find 'em!" Clay ordered in fair imitation of an old bounty hunter he had been watching. Yankee began eating the T-shirt. I turned away. Clay blushed. "Find 'em!" Clay ordered again as Yankee stood there looking silly with the corners of the T-shirt hanging out from under his jowls. He thought it was a great game. It was at least as much fun as showing.

Carefully and patiently Jim and Clay solved Yankee's problems. Within an hour Yankee had stopped eating wardrobes and had started looking for people. All dogs have a favorite reward and most handlers work on that system. One dog present expected a dill pickle at the end of a successful run. Clay and Jim worked things out with Yankee. He agreed on Milky Ways, with or without the paper wrapper.

For several days, in rain and in brilliant fall sunlight, Yankee and Clay ran up and down hills looking for policemen who offered themselves as bait. The same thing was going on all over the countryside. Anyone approaching earth for the first time and coming upon this scene from above would have thought the human race madder than it really is. Grown men were running and ducking behind trees and flopping on the ground while other grown men and a tall, lanky teenage kid were being dragged back and forth by enormous hounds. The object of the game, apparently, was for the dogs to wash the faces of the men who had flopped on the ground. But a lot of bloodhounds did get better at their job. Although it was never our intention that Yankee would put on a badge and become a full-time police officer, he at least learned a little more about his heritage. Yankee had found *his* roots. He had been bred to save man, woman, and child from their own folly. I managed to get a good television news report out of it with the camera crew from ABC who met me there. While everyone else ran, flopped, and followed, we filmed.

The Schodack adventure had an unexpected sequel. Shortly after we returned, exhausted, from the upstate countryside, I was asked to do a television special on dogs for ABC. The producer loved the idea of the bloodhound, and fully a quarter of the show was a recreation of the Schodack adventures. Once again Clay, Yankee, and Sgt. James Zarifis starred in a training sequence. Yankee still wanted to eat Jim's dirty T-shirt, but he settled for finding Jim instead. Yankee turned out to be as big a ham in front of the camera as he was in the show ring. He was less than wildly enthusiastic about man-hunting, but he loved the whole movie-making scene.

Nine

Yankee, like all fine athletes, must stay in good condition—or, as the English say, at the top of his form. He is expected to look and act his best at all times. You never know when you are going to be called upon when you are a star. Within a period of a few weeks, after he achieved his championship, Yankee appeared at the Westminster Kennel Club Show at Madison Square Garden, for three days running at a special exhibition in the lobby of a savings bank on Madison Avenue, on the Mike Douglas television show, and on "Good Morning America" on ABC. He loved it. He also posed for a magazine cover and a book jacket and sat for a portrait by a well-known artist, Arne Besser.

Diet is one of the most important elements in an athlete's regimen. Yankee eats carefully balanced meals. Although he does enjoy a small taste of chicken or roast beef now and then, he eats almost no table scraps and gets no junk food at all. To keep his teeth strong and clean he eats kibble flavored with a tablespoon or two of canned dog food—but only as a flavoring—or a little cottage cheese or a scrambled egg. Dogs must never eat raw eggs. They block their ability to absorb vitamins, so a dog regularly supplied with raw eggs could almost starve to death or at least lose weight and condition on the best of diets. An egg scrambled in margarine, though, is tasty and does dress up a kibble breakfast.

Yankee always eats all of his meal, slowly and sloppily. He also likes good long drinks of cold, clean water. He is rather like a camel: a drink takes twenty minutes. His ears hang into his food and water, of course;

if not caught in time, he walks around the house dribbling two trails from his ear tips. All bloodhound owners keep a towel on a hook near the kitchen door to dab and daub their pets after they have eaten and had a go at the water dish. The dogs come to expect it. I think it embarrasses them at first, but it becomes routine: *drink, slurp, drool, dab, daub, drink, slurp. . . .*

Yankee is kept at a measured 125 to 130 pounds. Some bloodhounds, like the mighty Limbo, can weigh 150 pounds or even a little more, but if Yankee were allowed to get that heavy he would appear gross and lose all his natural grace and beauty. His weight is maintained by diet control and exercise. Yankee loves his exercise. (You weigh a bloodhound by first weighing yourself, then picking the bloodhound up, stepping back on the scale, and having someone else read the dial for you. After you subtract your own weight to get your dog's weight you lie down for a long time waiting for your back to heal.)

There are eight dogs in the Caras household besides Yankee, and they all understand perfectly well what is said to them—when it serves their purposes to do so. For example, if I walk into the room, or if Clay does, and say, "Would you dogs like me to throw some . . . ?" The question never gets finished. There is a monumental explosion of canine enthusiasm and a herd of thundering dogs is out on the deck, leaping and caroming off each other. Yankee usually stands still, rolls his head back, and sends the most incredible notes rolling into the sky. Yes, indeed, they would like it very much if Clay or I would throw some . . .

The throwables, of course, are sticks, and the arena where the show takes place is on the beach which, fortunately, is just out the back door. Once the deck door is opened, all the dogs roar and thunder down the fourteen steps to their fenced-in yard. Anyone coming up the steps would be flattened, so a check is always made before the deck door is opened for the dogs, who collectively weigh an estimated 540 pounds.

Once in the fenced yard, the pack assembles at the beach-side metal gate and there then ensues a concert that sounds as if all the singers were being subjected to the fires of hell. Canine impatience is a noisy affair. In comparison, what follows the ringing of a recess bell at a grade school sounds like a religious retreat.

On the beach the whole pack goes berserk, pirouetting and leaping and shouting, Me! Me! Me! The sticks fly in all directions until my arm or Clay's gives out. The dogs thunder back and forth on the hard-packed sand, which is very good for their feet and legs, and anyone getting in the way will think they have participated in a seismic event. More than one guest has come out to watch the fun and misplaced his or her body. A bloodhound catching you behind the knees at twenty-five miles an hour can be very upsetting, literally. The most amazing display was put on by a guest who innocently joined the scene carrying a Scotch-on-the-rocks. He got it right behind the knees and his glass went straight up in the air. It also came straight down and our startled guest, now on his knees, caught it as it passed his nose. Some, but not all, of the Scotch was lost. It was a stunt one could never hope to repeat.

The stick-fetching part of Yankee's and the other dogs' exercise regimen led to a remarkable display of canine intelligence. Unfortunately, Yankee was bested.

When Yankee arrived on the scene Jeremy was already on deck and two and a half years old. Jeremy Boob, as he is called, is a perfectly magnificent golden retriever. He has one of the handsomest heads I have ever seen on a dog of his breed but, unfortunately, like so many goldens today, Jeremy Boob has a malformation of the hips called displasia. He can still function, but because he was obviously imperfect, we had him altered so he could not breed even by accident. It is believed by many dog authorities that displasia can be passed along from generation to generation. Early diet may also have a great deal to do with it. Jeremy came to us with his hips already whonky.

At any rate, Jeremy's heritage is that of the retrieving dog. That means he has excellent eyesight and a kind of computer in his head that permits him to see a stick go up (to him it is the same as a duck going by) and know exactly where it will fall to earth. It is an instantaneous calculation. Jeremy is always there to catch the falling stick or at least to be in a position to pounce on it. Yankee's heritage is in his nose. He can never imitate the retriever's visually oriented skill. But Yankee, the ever-willing dog, doesn't know this. When the sticks become airborne, Yankee *thinks* he is a retriever, too.

Jeremy is not only equipped with sharper eyes than Yankee—he is faster. No matter what Yankee would do as a puppy, Jeremy was always on top of the stick first. But time passed, and Yankee grew and grew and grew. At eight months he passed Jeremy in size. At a year he was larger, much stronger, and no longer awed by the fine mature male. Jeremy lost his dominance.

What then ensued once the stick flew was a mad dash to the impact zone led by Jeremy. Jeremy would get the stick only to find his way blocked by Yankee. He couldn't get past his friend the hound and return for a pat and some praise. It wasn't difficult for Yankee to wrest the stick away and come for the pat himself. Jeremy, the real stick finder, would stand there crestfallen. It was then that canine intelligence came into play. Jeremy thought it through and beat Yankee at his game.

Both dogs are males, which means they have an extra means of communication. When a male dog lifts his leg, a letter is sent—or a telex. At the very least a call is made.

Once a male dog lifts his leg, all other male dogs must acknowledge the message or territorial boundary marks (or perhaps it is just a simple "hello" or "hi, there"). The other males must do exactly the same thing in exactly the same place. It is very rude not to and possibly unwise, since it could mean a territory lost, or something, perhaps, we can't even understand.

The routine now became, stick in the air, dogs thundering, Jeremy on the stick, and then, very quickly, leg in the air. That stopped Yankee cold and he had to send his reply. The minute Jeremy was through, Yankee would step up and there he would be, leg high, looking silly and confused while Jeremy streaked for home with the stick. Poor Yankee never could figure out how to beat the rap. After all, stick fetching came into being only after men and dogs began living together. The pee signal goes all the way back to the wolf origin of the dog. Jeremy always heads for the water dish the moment the question about "would you like" nearly gets asked. He has had to turn himself into a water pistol in order to fulfill his destiny as a retriever.

Jeremy's name once caused a small stir. He was named Jeremy Boob by my daughter Pamela (who bought him with her earnings as a riding coach) after a character in the Beatles' movie *Yellow Submarine.* He wears a tag on his collar that states his name and our phone number. One day someone left a gate ajar and Jeremy wandered off. Long ago he discovered where the school bus stops and he does like to escape and wander up there late in the afternoon and wait for the kids to unload. It doesn't happen often, but when it does, it is kind of "shop for a kid," because Jeremy, like all good golden retrievers, loves children. He circulates among the kids as they pour off the bus and picks a good one to go home with. It has always been worth some good patting and often a cookie once the house is reached. He heads home after an hour or two, but we do not believe that dogs should go wandering, even on country roads. They belong on their own property where they can't get hurt or annoy other people.

That day, though, Jeremy did get out and pick himself up a kid-for-the-day. He evidently was admitted to the new and therefore interesting kitchen and did get his cookie. But when it was time for him to head for home (when the cookies ran out, probably) the temporarily adopted family did not feel he should be turned loose to wander again. Very kindly they examined his collar and found the tag stating the name Jeremy Boob and giving our phone number. Apparently the Jeremy part was a little hard to read. The tag, after all, wasn't exactly new.

Unfortunately my very English mother-in-law answered the phone. (She attended Mrs. Something-or-Other's School for the Daughters of Gentlemen in Henley-on-Thames and can say "I beg your pardon" as no one else on earth can. I think she majored in indignation.) The voice at the end of the line said, very clearly, "Hello, I have your Boob." My mother-in-law bristled and laid on a very heavy "I beg your . . ." Clay was sent to fetch the wayward Jeremy while I poured Mrs. Phyllis Langdon Barclay a Dubonnet Blanc on the rocks. Yankee went with

Clay and I am sure Jeremy gave him an earful in the back of the wagon on the way home. Jeremy got his own earful once he arrived back on his own turf. I know Jeremy still thinks about the school bus but the gate is now kept very carefully locked. "My boob, indeed!" my mother-in-law muttered later that evening. "Whatever do you suppose possessed the woman?" Fortunately, we keep one small sitting room in our house completely Victorian. Everything in it is from that remarkable era when Queen Victoria sat on the throne of England. I know Phyllis found it very comforting that evening.

Ten

Bloodhounds, as mentioned earlier, do not mature until they are about three years old—at least the dogs don't. Bitches usually mature much earlier, sometimes in half the time. When I say a male bloodhound doesn't mature, I mean he doesn't really have all his classical good looks. That comes with a full quota of bone, a full, broad chest, and that certain look almost middle-aged men get that is hopefully so irresistible to women.

Because they are not fully developed, bloodhounds, once they get their championship status, can be at a disadvantage for up to two years. Yankee, of course, had gone all the way by the time he was thirteen months. After that he couldn't compete against class dogs, but only dogs and bitches that were champions, too. In the dog show world they are referred to as *specials*. Since most specials on the show circuit at that time were mature, Yankee was at a disadvantage. It was, however, a disadvantage all large dogs of quality face at the same stage of life. They are the awkward, in-between years.

Jill and Clay decided that for the next twenty-three months Yankee would show only enough to keep in practice and, of course, satisfy his own ego. That ego had grown to such proportions that whenever he heard applause Yankee would throw his head up and put himself into a near approximation of the show stance. At the Manhattan Savings Bank lobby demonstrations, where he was invited to appear two years running, Yankee was greeted with applause and expressed his appreciation not only by posing like a cover-boy but by baying back at the audience. They thought that was grand and applauded some more. Yankee thought that that was grand, and so forth. It is a wonder he didn't set off the alarms.

Yankee's love of applause nearly caused an accident on one occasion. I was teaching a course one evening a week at the School of Veterinary Medicine of the University of Pennsylvania. One Tuesday Jill and I drove down to Philadelphia from New York, taking Yankee with us. I thought the veterinary students in the class might like to meet the big boy himself. It was a grand mix and Yankee circulated among the hundred and thirty-odd students, making friends and drooling on their knees and notebooks.

I frequently use guest lecturers in my course, and our lecturer that night was Phyllis Wright, a municipal animal control and shelter operations expert for The Humane Society of the United States in Washington. She had come up to share her expertise with my class. I introduced her in somewhat glowing terms because I do honestly admire her very much. (Several years earlier she had joined us on our annual African photographic safari, and she really is a wonderful person.)

As I finished my introductory remarks, Phyllis stepped up to the edge of the somewhat high platform at the front of the lecture hall and was greeted by applause. Yankee, in the back of the room, heard the applause and, with a mighty roar of total agreement, shot down the aisle and up onto the stage. He bounded to the front edge and began posing. Unfortunately, Phyllis was in his way and she very nearly went up, off, and over. Phyllis was forgiving, the class was delighted, and Yankee was sent to the back of the hall in disgrace. He still has the ego problem. He simply cannot resist applause. He just can't believe it isn't for him. It would never do to take him to the theater. He would be very disruptive.

What do you do with a dog that is a champion, cannot appear in dog shows to any real advantage, and has already done the top television talk shows? After all, how much can even a champion bloodhound have to say to America? One thing you can do with such a dog is allow him to become a father.

A word of explanation is in order here. Yankee is the only dog we have ever bred, and there have been a lot of dogs. There is a tragic surplus of pet dogs and cats in the United States, and the puppies and kittens that must be killed every year number between thirteen and fifteen million! We have always thought it a crime to add to this surplus and so, no matter how much we thought of a pet, we never let them contribute to that tragic problem. A superb example of a pure-bred animal is something else, however. A dog like a bloodhound is not only an animal, it is a part of human history. It is, in the eyes of many, a work of art and as a genetic accomplishment it is a scientific marvel. If nobody bred bloodhounds, a breed that came into being when Rome almost ruled the world would vanish within fifteen years. That would be terrible! It has been our belief that only an animal whose genetic potential was really needed by its breed should be allowed to create a new generation. Clay's Yankee was the first dog we owned of whom we felt that was true. Yankee agreed.

Jill consulted with the Sinkinsons, and it was decided that the lovely Ch. The Rectory's Litany would become Yankee's mate, when next she came into heat. Although they were related, they were far enough apart that the amount of inbreeding involved would not be harmful. People are often confused about inbreeding. It is not necessarily bad, and fine lines of dogs are often achieved by a certain amount of close breeding during the formative stages. The Sinkinson line—The Rectory dogs— did not need it, though, so Yankee's mate-to-be was chosen in part by her position on the family tree. Close, but not too close.

One June morning, at six-thirty, the call came. Litany, or Tanny as she is called, was ready to meet her mate. The trouble was that her mate was with us in East Hampton, New York, and she was with the Sinkinsons in their summer place outside Farmington, Maine. It was close to a ten-hour drive. But there was no stopping Jill. Clay couldn't get away because of his job at the veterinary hospital and I was about to leave on a lecture tour. Jill barged into her mother's room and invited her to go on the great northern trek. My mother-in-law demurred and Jill shrugged and muttered something about falling asleep at the wheel with no one to talk to and being demolished in a wreck. Jill, her mother, and Yankee left for Maine within the hour. Sex is a powerful imperative, as we all know. Yankee had no idea of what was expected of him. He didn't even know he was engaged.

Apparently my mother-in-law did not realize what breeding fine dogs entails. They are not turned loose into a yard and allowed to handle things naturally. It is a carefully orchestrated performance that lasts up to forty-five minutes. My mother-in-law had taken a needlepoint project along and set to work furiously on her pillow trying not to appear in the least interested in the sordid details of puppy making. This, by the way, at a quarter to midnight. There are certain days when the female is most likely to conceive and Jackie and Jill did not want to waste one of them. After driving for almost eleven hours, Jill joined right in. With Jackie roaring advice, encouragement, and instructions, and with Jill, bleary-eyed from the drive, on hand, Yankee and Tanny did their bit for the future of the bloodhound kind. Yankee was a good sport and cooperated.

As it turned out, my mother-in-law apparently was not as disinterested as she would have had everyone believe. She did a whole section of her pillow upside down and later had to pull it all out stitch by stitch. She had some wholly unbelievable explanation of how and why the needlepoint fiasco had occurred, but we knew the truth. She was peeking.

On each of three consecutive days Yankee and Tanny were mated. From then on, as is always the case, the matter is in someone else's hands. Jill and her mother and a very pleased if somewhat weary dog drove back to Long Island. Yankee would assume a new personality, we knew, for now he was a stud. He would have to be watched, especially with Jeremy.

In a couple of weeks Jackie called. Tanny was expecting. The breeding had taken. Within sixty-four days of the first breeding there would be the first litter of Yankee's puppies. We all kept our fingers crossed and raised high. It was to be a major happening.

Yankee surprised us all. He growled at Jeremy a few times, but a wooden cooking spoon on the rump works wonders. His applause hang-up we could live with, but not a big-stud-on-campus attitude. Yankee got the message. Although he would still prefer not to have strange male dogs come onto the grounds, he and Jeremy are just fine. Jeremy (Boob) is too much of a gentleman anyway. He is not a squabbler and neither really is the mighty Yank. Despite his glorious success in all endeavors (except retrieving), Yankee is a pleasant fellow to have around.

Jackie kept Jill informed (almost day by day) as Litany progressed in her pregnancy. Dr. Bob Patterson, the veterinarian who had delivered Yankee by Caesarean section, was in the process of moving from Maryland to Maine, too, but he was not yet on hand. Another veterinarian, although he was not really familiar with bloodhounds, seemed to have the matter under control. Regular examinations showed that Tanny was not only going to have puppies, she was going to have a lot of them. Bloodhound bitches have a lot of room inside and generally have large litters. Ten is not unusual.

On August 12, 1976, Yankee's mate delivered the first Yankee litter. The number was ten, but sadly the survivors were quickly reduced to seven. In the original litter there were four males and six females. Three of the males were not destined to survive. One was born imperfect and died naturally before the first day was out. That can happen, especially with young bitches. Unhappily, Tanny did the terrible roll-over-and-be-bored number and smothered another male. The third male developed a small infection, and the standby veterinarian misdiagnosed the ailment. Before the mistake was discovered, it was too late, and the third male died. The one surviving male was named The Rectory's Prodigal Son. Later, when Yankee met him, he embarrassed his father. For some reason, Yankee couldn't look at him. He hung his head and turned away. There was no reason for Yankee to be embarrassed, for Prodigal Son, or Digger, as he is called since he thinks kennel run fences are for digging under, has gone on to become at times during his young career the top winning bloodhound in America. He is a magnificent big dog, even larger than his father.

There is an important point to be made with Digger's success. Great dogs, like great horses, are rated not only by their success in the show ring or on the track but also by their success as studs. Man o' War, one of the greatest Thoroughbreds ever to come out of Kentucky and probably the most famous horse that ever lived, never won the Kentucky Derby. What made him so famous was that when he sired foals his stamp was upon them. He was the source of superior genetic material. And that, apparently, is true of Yankee. Even if he never appeared in a show again he has proved the final point he has to prove. He is a great stud. His six daughters proved to be all superior champion stock following in the footsteps of their one surviving brother, the great Prodigal Son.

One other point about Digger. He is as sweet as his father. One weekend Jackie and Sink were in town for a show and we suggested that they and Digger stay with us in the city apartment. Jill and I woke up in the morning to find a one-hundred-pound-plus male bloodhound puppy asleep between us with his head on Jill's pillow and all four feet straight up in the air. He is a mighty pussycat of a dog, but since he is also a stud now, he and Yankee tend to grumble at each other. Once dogs are grown, two huge studs are generally best kept apart. Individually, though, Yankee and Digger are two of the sweetest-natured dogs I have ever known. It is nice to know that that is also being passed along in Yankee's genes, not just cover-boy good looks.

Eleven

The six girls in Yankee's first litter have been more than interesting. Because Yankee's real name is Yankee Patriot, the litter was a "P" litter. Like Prodigal Son, each of the female names begins with that letter. There are Piety, Pax, Propaganda, Pilgrim, Purgatory, and Peter's Pence. They each have call names as well, of course.

Purgatory is known as Tory, and has gone to live with Mr. and Mrs. Frank Gilbert in Phoenix, Arizona. Mrs. Gilbert is the actress Amanda Blake, who for over nineteen years appeared on the television show "Gunsmoke" as Miss Kitty. Amanda and Frank have a private wild animal breeding compound where they do research to help save endangered species. They also have a lot of dogs and cats. Tory basks in her glory with Keemo the Lion and seventeen cheetahs. (The Gilberts were among the first to crack the mysterious cheetah breeding system—one female to a number of males.) There is a large swimming pool in a yard surrounded by a high wall. We have visited Tory there, and, like the true daughter of a king, she is living very well indeed. Like all bloodhounds, Tory takes her high life-style for granted. There aren't very many bloodhounds in Arizona, so it is hard to find a show that is a major. Tory is showing well, though, and is getting her points. She will shortly have a Ch. in front of her name, as well.

Four of her sisters are already champions. Piety, Pax, Propaganda, and Pilgrim "finished" very quickly which, again, means became champions. The sixth sister, Peter's Pence, was to be a different story.

It is not at all usual for the owner of a bitch to give a puppy to the owner of the stud. A stud fee is paid, and that is almost always very much less than a puppy is worth. Because Jackie and Jill had become such good friends and because the Sinkinsons thought so highly of Yankee, they agreed that from the Yankee-Tanny breeding, Jill could select a puppy. It was a most unusual arrangement and not one I think the Sinkinsons will ever repeat. It was so unusual that they decided no matter which puppy Jill selected, it would be called Peter's Pence. Peter's Pence is the tithe or fee-contribution that every Roman Catholic church pays to the Vatican each year. You might know that an Episcopalian priest would come up with that! It was intended, no doubt, to make the Carases feel guilty.

Peter's Pence got the obvious call name of Penny and joined the Caras pack when she was ten weeks old. She was a very beautiful puppy, and it was clear that she was yet another Sinkinson hound (and Yankee puppy) and could go all the way. At first Yankee thought she was the worst idea he had ever met. She pulled on his ears, pulled on his tail, tried to eat out of his food dish, and generally made a pain of herself. (It is strange, but in a household full of dogs bloodhounds somehow know that they are of the same kind. Yankee and Penny in time were to become very, very close. Siamese cats, we have noticed, do the same thing.)

Fortunately for Yankee, Pamela was in town one day about a month before Penny was born. She met a little boy pushing a wheelbarrow and crying. The barrow was full of puppies of somewhat casual origin and the boy sobbed that his father had told him that if he didn't find homes for the puppies by one o'clock that afternoon the father would drown all that were left. Pamela, shocked by the unknown man's monstrous treatment of his child and puppies, made a deal to meet the boy at quarter to one. Pamela would take what was left in the wheelbarrow. It never occurred to her that the boy might have been a budding Barrymore. At any rate, since it happened to be the Fourth of July the little black bitch Pamela *saved* was named Liberty, or Libby. She was to become Penny's very close friend, and she helped Yankee to survive the original onslaught of an exuberant bloodhound puppy bitch.

Penny, like Digger and the other puppies, was both beautiful and extremely pleasant. She is, in fact, one of the very nicest dogs I have ever known. At six months she appeared in her first show, and, although somewhat less enthusiastic than her father had been at that age, she did very well. From the very start she began winning.

Jill thought it would be great fun to have Penny finish, achieve her championship, in Madison Square Garden, at the great Westminster Kennel Club Show. There was every indication that she could take her class and go Winner's Bitch. That would give her the points she needed to become a champion, too. She already had won her two majors, and Westminster, certainly a major, would make it three! As February approached, Jill held Penny back. She did not want her to become a champion before the big show at the Garden, for then she could only go up against the other champions or specials. She was much too young to make a showing against the world-famous champions, some of them five and six years old, who would be there for the greatest dog show event of the year.

Some weeks before the show Penny had gone through her second heat, the period during which she could breed. Periods last twenty-one days and occur every six months in a normal healthy bitch. We were very careful during her heat to keep her apart from Yankee, the only Caras dog capable of mating with her. Now that she was grown, Yankee had no way of knowing that she was his daughter, and it wouldn't have bothered him in the slightest had he known. He was a stud, and she was a bitch, and in heat she would have proven irresistible.

One evening Jill and I attended a dinner party. Everyone in the house had an engagement that evening and when Jill and I got home Yankee and Penny were standing side by side at the top of the stairs to greet us. Someone had left a latch unlatched or a hook unhooked. There was no doubt in our minds about what must have happened while we were out. We certainly did not want Penny heavy with puppies at Westminster and we did not want her to have puppies by her own father. That kind of breeding is sometimes done, as I indicated earlier, but there is no justification in the case of these two dogs. The Rectory line does not need that kind of reinforcing.

What to do? A quick rush to the telephone. The Caras dogs have three veterinarians: Dr. Herbert French, Dr. Dale Tarr, and Dr. Thomas Rothwell. All three attend to the pack at their hospital in East Hampton, although Tom Rothwell has a special interest in bloodhounds. Tom listened to Jill's frantic tale of sexual mishap and announced that he would be right over.

There was no reasonable way to tell if a breeding had taken place, but Tom explained that there was a shot he could give Penny that would stop things before they got started. He did explain, in all fairness, that in a very, very small percentage of the cases there could be a bad side effect to the shot, but it was *rarely* seen. I don't think we even listened to that part of it, which proved to be a terrible mistake. Penny got the shot right then and there (and was scheduled for another a few days later). Then Jill, Tom, and I settled down in the Victorian sitting room for a late-night bit of sociability. Yankee, Penny, and a few of the other animals wandered in (they adore their doctors and a veterinarian coming to dinner or being visited at the hospital is greeted with great affectionate displays). Tom sipped his drink and muttered something to Yankee about being ashamed of himself. Yankee thumped his tail. Tom's sense of propriety didn't worry him in the slightest. Yankee wasn't ashamed at all.

The Westminster Kennel Club Show always takes place on a Monday and Tuesday in February. Jill and I moved Yankee and Penny in from the country the Friday before to let them rest up at the apartment. They would get their final baths there and their nails would get the final trimming. Something was bothering Jill, though, something she felt was not quite right.

On Saturday she remarked that Penny was depressed. Jill felt it, and the feeling was not to be ignored. Real animal people, I am absolutely certain, communicate with animals on levels and in ways other people do not understand. I can't define it, animal people never can. It is just there. Lion trainers know their cats, mahouts know their elephants, horse people know their mounts, and dog and cat people know their companion animals in ways that simply defy description. In our family Jill and Pamela have the gift. Clay and I are good practical animal lovers and handlers and perhaps something of naturalists, but our practical, scientific approach is different from the intuitiveness of Jill and Pamela. They sense animals.

Several times Saturday night Jill got up to check on Penny. She slept, Jill did not. On Sunday morning Jill repeated her misgivings. Penny was not happy. Something was wrong. As the day passed, if Penny's condition did not deteriorate, Jill's did.

By early afternoon I concurred. We had better move fast. Our first concern was Penny's well-being. We were also concerned because she was due to be in Madison Square Garden early the next morning.

We are fortunate in New York City in having the Animal Medical Center. It is one of the finest veterinary hospitals in the world. Young graduate veterinarians from all over the world try to get an internship at AMC, for it is there that the leading specialists gather. There are veterinary bone specialists, eye specialists, and neurologists, men and women who could not afford to specialize at any place but AMC, Angell Memorial in Boston (run by the MSPCA), and a few other centers scattered around the world.

The Chief of Services at AMC is Dr. William Kaye, and I called him. He was out and couldn't be reached for hours. I called the veterinarian in charge that weekend, and he told me to bring Penny in right away. A young veterinarian who was very highly recommended, Dr. Bob Cohen, examined her and, although he couldn't spot anything in a gross examination, agreed with Jill that a more careful study was indicated. Penny was led off for x-rays and blood tests. She wasn't even walking right. Her head was down and she shuffled. She didn't look back at us. Jill and I settled down for a miserable wait while Dr. Cohen called upstairs and said he wanted an emergency put on the tests he had ordered.

Within an hour we learned that Penny's white cell count was off and there were other indications, too, that Jill's gut reaction had been accurate. More tests, another hour-long wait, and then Dr. Cohen appeared without Penny.

"There is a strong likelihood that it is pyometra." Our hearts sank. Pyometra is a massive abscess of the uterus. It is one of the almost never seen, possible side effects of the shot Tom Rothwell had given Penny, and about which he had felt it his duty to warn us. The trouble is, pyometra is virtually untreatable. The only thing usually attempted is an emergency spaying, by a specialist when possible. Spaying not only meant no puppies from the lovely Penny but no more showing either. Even more important was that Penny's life would certainly be in danger if Dr. Cohen's diagnosis was right.

A word about why Penny could not be shown if she had to be spayed. The whole idea of the dog show, aside from the fact that it has become a major sporting event, is to select by elimination the very best animals of each breed. It is those animals that people want puppies from and those animals that are bred. Thus the breed is maintained and gradually improved. If a dog or bitch cannot be bred, the original purpose of the show is negated. Spayed bitches can be shown in obedience competition (something that is growing in popularity), but not in regular shows for points and championship recognition.

It was clear that Penny would not appear at Madison Square Garden with her father the next morning. At that point all we wanted was for her to live. Pyometra, like polio and diphtheria in the past, is a word that can strike terror to the heart.

Jill had a very special relationship with Penny. There existed between them something that had made it possible for Jill to know by intuition that Penny was not right inside, although even a skilled veterinarian could not find anything on first examination. To Dr. Bob Cohen's credit, he was intuitive enough to pay attention to Jill's intuition.

Penny was placed in an intensive care unit. That meant that a nurse would be with her all through the afternoon and night. A veterinarian would also be full-time in the unit and a blood test would be done every hour, night and day. Data received from the tests would be fed into a computer. The most recent veterinary diagnostic technology would be used. We could do nothing more. It would have been wrong to go up and see Penny. She was sedated and with her nurse, and was being checked every few minutes by a veterinarian as well. If she saw us she would want to leave with us. We left feeling very dejected indeed.

On the way back to the apartment, Jill muttered, "It just isn't fair." I knew what she meant. She and Penny had quite literally worked together. There had been nail care, coat care, diet, exercise, obedience training, those early dog shows when Penny behaved like a plate of worms on four legs. Through all of that Jill had been building this bitch into a perfect specimen in perfect health so that she would be able to carry on the great Yankee tradition and establish Jill's own kennel name. She wasn't even a champion yet because of Jill's quite natural desire to see her finish in the Garden. Now, poor Penny lay on a pile of clean towels being attended by the best veterinary skills available on earth, but with no certainty that she would even live.

That night Jill spent a lot of time hugging Yankee and crying into his great neck. He stood very still and listened. One would swear that he understood.

We called Dr. Cohen several times, and it was clear that he was personally supervising the case even though a specialist had taken over. I understood what he meant when Bill Kaye, his boss, later described Bob Cohen as one of the outstanding young veterinarians around. In the meantime Tom Rothwell was calling in from East Hampton at regular intervals—both to us and to the AMC—to get reports. He, too, like most people who knew her, had a very special relationship with Penny.

At midnight the veterinarian on duty called Bob Cohen at home. There were stronger signs, now, that pyometra was the correct diagnosis and an enormous abscess was threatening Penny's life. It was decided the surgeon had better be consulted. At twelve-fifteen he was called out of bed and by one A.M. he was at Penny's side. The men reviewed the computer read-outs and decided it could go until morning, but no longer. The surgeon wanted his regular surgical team and not an emergency night crew for what was likely to prove to be a difficult and dangerous operation. Penny had already made friends at AMC. We later learned that no matter how sick she was she always thumped her tail and tried to get up to greet whoever came near her cage. A nurse did sit with her all night patting and reassuring her. Penny was a very sick dog.

I had been told to call by nine o'clock in the morning for an update.

We arrived at Madison Square Garden with Yankee at eight and I got Jill and the big champ settled in and headed for the press office. At exactly nine I called the AMC. Dr. Cohen came on the phone and told me the bad news. Pyometra had been confirmed. There was an experimental technique, developed in Texas, whereby both horns of a large bitch's uterus can be implanted with tubes and constant flushing applied. It is sometimes successful, often leaves a dog sterile anyway, but, most importantly, was very hard on the animal and can fail. That is, the dog might die. That was out as of then and there. What did Bob Cohen think we should do?

His answer was without equivocation: "I think you should give permission for us to spay her."

"When will you do it?" I asked.

"Within twenty minutes. They are waiting for her in surgery now."

I gave permission, from a phone booth in Madison Square Garden, where we had hoped to see Penny become a champion that very day. When I arrived back down in the bench area Jill was sitting with Yankee, who was still being as sympathetic as he knew how to be. I think he was confused because Penny wasn't with him. Jill stood up when she saw me coming. She knew. That intuition again.

While Penny was being operated on uptown, a number of friends and fellow bloodhound enthusiasts gathered around to offer their sympathy. It was a time for friends, and our friends were there. Jackie and Sink were particularly supportive. At eleven-thirty I called again. Penny had come out of surgery, was in intensive care again, and would live.

When news of Penny's sad condition got around, one bloodhound breeder was seen to smile and heard to say to his wife, "Whew, that's one less bitch we have to worry about." Several other breeders offered to kill him for us but we suggested that he be ignored. He was, by everybody. His grossness and lack of feeling underscored again the diversity of people who own and show dogs. They run from the best to the worst friends and acquaintances you can have.

About a week after Penny got home from the hospital she passed out one very snowy Saturday evening. Her gums and lips were gray instead of a healthy pink. I was away on a lecture tour and a real blizzard was shaping up. Jill did the usual—called Tom Rothwell. Before she had even finished her sentence Tom ordered, "Meet me at the hospital."

Tom arrived dressed for a dinner party and spent no more than five minutes with Penny before heading for the phone. He told his wife to go without him and guided Jill and Penny to the car. "You pat, I'll drive." Penny was on her way back to the Animal Medical Center 120 miles away.

At AMC later that night, the veterinarians on duty were able to run tests that could not be run in the hospital Tom shared with Dale Tarr, Herb French, and Al Pontic, the three senior veterinarians in the practice. Indeed, no normal veterinary hospital can offer anything like the procedures available at AMC.

Late that night, as the snow piled up and the plows worked, Tom drove a very worried Jill all the way back to East Hampton. The next day, Sunday, Bob Cohen made a special trip despite the foul weather. Penny, after all, was his patient, too. Two days later the scare had passed. Penny needed some general building up, but she could go home to convalesce with Yankee and her friends in the country. Penny got better, and very quickly the whole terrible episode was behind us. She can't have puppies, she can't appear in shows, she will never have Ch. in front of her name, but Penny, daughter of Yankee and his very best friend, will be a champion to all of us forever.

Twelve

No bitch can ever unseat Penny in the Caras household, but Yankee does have to have a mate if his beauty and charm are ever to be established in a line all his own. So another mate has been obtained, a distant cousin from Farmington, Maine. Her name is The Rectory's Trinity—Tee for short—and she has all the charisma the first two Caras-owned bloodhounds have. She also thinks she is a retriever, although she is no better at it than Yankee and Penny are. She, too, has been caught up in the spirit of Jeremy Boob, though she will never match his skill. Libby is Tee's friend as well as Penny's, but Yankee has a strange reaction to that.

As Penny began to mature, and before the unlatched door led to Penny's travail, Yankee became very possessive of her. He did not appreciate other dogs becoming too familiar with her. When Penny and Libby would get to playing their roughneck games Yankee would stand tall and square and bay. He was not pleased. Now he is doing that with Tee. At first she was as terrible an idea as the puppy Penny had been, he thought, but now Tee is growing and she is a bitch and Yankee the stud is doing his pack leader, Alpha dog number again. Only this time he is supposed to breed with Tee. With Penny it had been a careless door closer. Yankee watches Tee. Somehow, as each week passes, she seems less like a terrible idea and more like an interesting one.

Something should be said about the Caras dogs and their cats. I say *their* cats because, in fact, there is a certain possessiveness involved. The Peaceable Kingdom, as it exists in East Hampton, consists of nine cat-loving dogs and five dog-loving cats who match them. I don't know why it is, but that is true of all our animals.

Sometimes, of course, instinct does take over. One day recently, while Jill and I were exercising the pack with a skyful of soaring sticks, Daisy the cat came down to watch the fun. Penny and Libby got carried away with themselves and chased poor Daisy into some bushes. There was no question of them hurting her, but since they were chasing each other, why not chase something else, especially something small and fast?

A very sharp command brought Penny and Libby to their senses and to our sides looking very sheepish. Jill went and retrieved Daisy, who was sitting in some thick bushes washing herself, no doubt in an effort to calm her nerves. Jill carried Daisy down to where Libby and Penny sat looking dejected and ashamed. They both walked over and licked Daisy, all the while looking up at Jill with big sorrowful eyes. I think Daisy would rather have been chased than doused in dog spit, but the dogs, clearly, had gotten the message.

On winter evenings the cats single out a dog. Anything as large as a bloodhound or a golden retriever, of course, makes a grand hot water bottle. It is quite usual for each dog to be asleep more or less near the fireplace with a cat curled up in their paws. Some of the cats like to bathe the dogs and a colorpoint shorthair named Kate (the colorpoint shorthair was arrived at by crossing Siamese and tiger tabbies, and it eventually became a breed by itself) does not approve of bloodhound body odor. But Kate does love the dogs themselves. She is the one who washes and washes and washes the most. A dog weighing almost 130 pounds is a terrible undertaking for one cat tongue, but Kate keeps at it hour after weary hour. I don't think she is ever going to get a bloodhound to smell anything but like a bloodhound, yet I am sure she will keep on trying until the day she dies.

Some of our cats (most in fact), like some of our dogs, are strays, waifs, orphans that had to become part of our clan because the alternative was unacceptable to us. That means, inevitably, that some of the kittens lost their mothers too early. Anyone who has had cats knows what happens when a kitten does not nurse enough. The cat will suck and knead the rest of its life. It embarrasses Yankee and Jeremy very much that a couple of cats get to feeling very kittenish on a cozy winter night by the fire. They apparently think Jeremy and the Yank are their mothers. Yankee lies there looking humiliated while a cat tries to nurse on him and wiggles her toes against his ribs in a kneading action. Of course, there is no profit in it for the cat, except contentment of a peculiar kind, and for Yankee—as far as I can tell—he just hopes no one is looking.

Bloodhounds are not common in New York, and big handsome specimens are likely to draw stares and comments. Yankee always does; people often walk up and ask what kind of dog he is. Usually they are amazed to find how sweet and gentle the big hounds are because they have been brought up on the fictional nonsense tales of man-hunting packs. Very often, when he is in public, Yankee is recognized.

A couple of years ago *The New York Times Magazine* wanted a story about a fine show dog, and I wrote a piece about Clay and Yankee. Yankee ended up on the cover in a super portrait that many people, we have heard, cut out and framed. Unfortunately, there is a picture inside of Jill, Pamela, Yankee, and me that could understandably be captioned "Patty Hearst and her Kidnappers." The pictures of Clay and Yankee are fine, but the rest of us came off like Halloween partygoers. That portrait of Yankee made him the best-known bloodhound in America, and then there was a second shot at portrait fame.

The best dog photographer in America today, I am sure, and certainly one of the greatest who ever lived, is Alton Anderson of Rockland County, New York. He approached Jill at a dog show one day and said he had been looking for some outstanding bloodhounds to add to his portfolio of classic dog studies. Early one morning Jill drove Penny and Yankee up to Alton's studio and hundreds of photos were taken inside the studio and outside where the dogs could play in a small lake, something bloodhounds love to do. The portraits that resulted were classic examples of Alton Anderson's art, and a year or so later, when

Howell Book House published a book called *The Complete Bloodhound* by Catherine F. Brey, Yankee's face filled the front cover (and a snapshot I had taken of him appeared on the back cover). And a year after that, when I edited the first edition of Stoeger's *Dog Owner's Bible,* Yankee again appeared in the first photograph in the book.

All of this has added up to more fame and recognition. Wherever he goes, he is likely to be recognized. Not long ago Clay was walking Yankee on one of his rare visits to the city and some schoolboys came running up. "Is that Yankee?" they asked. Puzzled, Clay assured them it was. As they all gathered around him, patting him on the head and examining his acres of ears, they informed Clay that they had read about him in a reader or primary school magazine that has national distribution. That was some publicity that we—and Yankee—hadn't even known about. Yankee, we are sure, was quite pleased. He loves to be recognized. When you are recognized, you are usually patted. For it all, Yankee is still a dog, and being patted is what it is all about.

AFTERWORD

If you have read this far you have probably got the message that the Carases love animals. We do. We also love people, and we find that animals and people together are a very special combination. There are marvelous things that can happen when the mix is a good one.

I have often heard the criticism that animal lovers lavish too much time and money on their four-legged pets and that the money should be spent on children instead. Very often the people leveling that criticism are wearing terribly expensive fur coats, or jewelry, or are driving big, expensive cars. They also go to auctions and sales rooms and spend large sums on things that they find beautiful, things to grace their homes and lives. Why is it a good idea to hang diamonds around your neck while criticizing someone else for spending a fraction as much money on their hobbies? In fact, each of us does indulge himself or herself to some degree. That is what working hard is all about. I find diamonds cold while I find bloodhounds very warm.

I do not recommend bloodhounds as pets for the average home. I am asked about them often in that regard, and I always give the same answer. There are about 140 breeds and varieties of dogs recognized by the American Kennel Club, and some of them are nice all-around dogs—to name a few, beagles, spaniels, Boston terriers, golden and Labrador retrievers. Others, like bloodhounds, mastiffs, Danes, and borzois, are for special situations. They are too much work, too much care for most people. The happy pet and the happy pet owner are the result of careful matching. You should not get more dog than you can properly handle or care for. Bloodhounds should never be a person's first dog. Only when people have proven (to themselves, most important of all) that they are fully committed dog people, should the big hounds be attempted. They demand too much.

As for Yankee today? He is as happy as a clam, although I doubt very much that clams can ever be as happy as a dog. He has Penny with him and now Tee. He is waiting for Tee to grow up. She will become a champion (she is very beautiful) and have his puppies. He has the other dogs, too, and the cats and very good health. Dr. Tom Rothwell stops by at least once a week and visits with everyone. He gets licked from top to bottom (we can't even imagine how interesting a veterinarian must smell to a dog, especially a bloodhound) and the dogs and cats get a quick check.

Yankee leads the good life. He deserves to. He has never offered anything but love in this world, and, as far as we can tell, there is no end to his supply.

INDEX

The Author

Roger A. Caras is a widely known naturalist who has published over thirty books and numerous articles in national publications. A native of Methuen, Massachusetts, and a graduate of the University of Southern California, Los Angeles, his interest in nature and animals led to his traveling throughout the world and becoming a prominent conservationist. Besides writing and lecturing, Caras presently is a correspondent for ABC-TV Network News specializing in animals.